Jacob Redsecker

Across the continent

Jacob Redsecker

Across the continent

ISBN/EAN: 9783337257385

Printed in Europe, USA, Canada, Australia, Japan

Cover: Foto ©Andreas Hilbeck / pixelio.de

More available books at **www.hansebooks.com**

LETTERS

WRITTEN TO

THE CHURCH ADVOCATE,

DURING THE SUMMER OF 1879.

BY J. H. REDSECKER.

TO
THE MEMBERS OF
THE PACIFIC INSTITUTE EXCURSION,
WITH WHOM I MADE THE TOUR
ACROSS THE CONTINENT,
AND TO THE
FRIENDS IN CALIFORNIA
WHO RECEIVED US SO CORDIALLY AND
TREATED US SO KINDLY, THIS LITTLE
VOLUME IS RESPECTFULLY
DEDICATED.

INTRODUCTION.

As I may never have another opportunity of communicating with you, dear reader, I want to take you into my confidence and tell you a secret. I have longed to write a book. Indeed it has been the ambition of my life, haunting me like a horrible nightmare. I have not done so for several reasons. It was not for want of time, for I had all the time there is—twenty-four hours in every day, and where is the person who has more? Neither was it from fear of the book reviewers, for only a few persons read what they say, and soon forget it. You may, then, wonder why I did not write it. I'll tell you. A lack of ability alone prevented me from fulfilling a long cherished desire, as it doubtless has many others. I was conscious, too, that it would be difficult to find a publisher willing to assume the risk of its publication, or persons credulous enough to purchase the book. Do you wonder any longer?

The Poet Longfellow has beautifully said we should

"Learn to labor and to wait."

I have done so. I have labored unceasingly and waited patiently, and

"With a heart for any fate"

have ventured upon the sea of literature. The hour of my triumph has come; the measure of my ambition is full. I have made a book—and it isn't much of a book to boast of after all.

Be assured of this, the reviewers will not get hold of it to praise it, nor will the public have an opportunity of wasting effort in an attempt to purchase it. Let me tell you how I came to write it.

Two years ago, when in California, the Rev. Dr. Vincent suggested holding two Sunday-school Assemblies in the State—one in the Yosemite Valley, and the other on the Pacific Coast, at Monterey. The suggestion was cordially seconded by the California State Sunday-school Association, and the arrangements for the Assemblies placed in its hands. As the time approached, arrange-

PREFACE.

ments were made in the east to convey about a car-load of excursionists to the Assemblies, but the excursion grew on the hands of the management, so that it numbered over three hundred tourists. It was my good fortune to be a member of this Pacific Institute Excursion, which crossed the continent to attend these Assemblies, and to see the wonders of California. Now, it isn't every person that goes to California. It is an event in one's life; something to boast of, you know. At the request of friends I resolved to write letters descriptive of my travels to the *Church Advocate*, published in Harrisburg, Pa., and let the readers—to whom I am not an entire stranger—know something about the Excursion, the Assemblies, and the wonders of our country.

When the letters were written it was not my purpose to republish them; but a number of the tourists requesting copies of the papers containing my correspondence, and being unable to supply them, I determined to re-publish them in this more convenient and permanent form, as a memento of our travels, for private gratuitous circulation among the tourists and personal friends.

Some additional matter has been added of interest to the tourists, which was withheld for want of space in the over-crowded columns of a weekly paper.

I have written only of that which I saw and heard. In the language of Thomas de Quincy I would say: "Let him (the reader) read the sketch as belonging to one who wishes to be profoundly anonymous." If, therefore, there is anything deserving condemnation, please remember it was written by one who wishes to be "profoundly anonymous." If, on the contrary, there is anything in the letters that is particularly pleasing, the reader will oblige me by turning to the title-page, and remembering who wrote it.

I hope the letters will recall many pleasing incidents to the members of the Pacific Institute Excursion, and be of interest to those who have never made the tour "Across the Continent."

LEBANON, PA.   J. H. R.

ACROSS THE CONTINENT.

NUMBER ONE.

STARTING—THE WEST PENNSYLVANIA CONVENTION—DRIVING ACROSS THE COUNTRY, &C.

CHICAGO, May 26, 1879.

I don't know whether we are indebted to Samuel Bowles or Schuyler Colfax for originating the expression [Across the Continent] which heads this correspondence, but certain it is that Solomon was quite right when he said, "There is no new thing under the sun." Old ideas are taken up, revamped, and sent forth clothed in new language, but nevertheless, they are the same old things after all.

Dr. Dio Lewis, in his book called "Our Digestion," gives some excellent advice, which, if followed, will have a tendency to make well people sick and send sick people to their graves, while their friends are left to mourn their untimely death and inherit their "portable property," as Mr. Wemmick—he with the "post office of a mouth"—alliteratively called it. Dr. Lewis advises, in the book just mentioned, that fat people shall keep "their eyes open and their mouths shut;" and when I finally decided to become a member of the "Pacific Institute Excursion," with its high-sounding title, and still higher purpose of combining instruction with travel, I resolved, for once, to follow the doctor's advice,—at least in part. I resolved to keep not only my eyes open, but my ears, too, with a mental reservation about the mouth. I resolved I would see and hear all I could and write it out for *The Advocate*. Whether it will be edifying and instructive will remain an open question. With that, however, I have nothing to do. And now, having said this much by way of preface, let me begin at the beginning.

When the West Pennsylvania brethren arranged for their Sunday-school convention, I hadn't "California on the brain," and so promised to be with them, as did Elder Sigler, of *The Gem*. He, accompanied by Elder A. H. Long, left on the 20th inst., and was present from the beginning to the close. It was my misfortune to get there only for the afternoon and evening of the last day, and so I missed all the good things that had been said previously. Of one thing I am certain, they lost nothing by my absence.

The convention was held in Harmony, Butler county, a quaint old town built seventy years ago by George Rapp, the founder of the community now residing at Economy. George Rapp, accompanied by his nephew Frederick, who was also his adopted son, came to this country from Wurtemburg, Germany, in 1804, and settled on the Connoquenessing creek in Butler county. Here he purchased nearly eight thousand acres of land. He had about eight hundred men and women colonists with him. The first year was one of privation, and about half of the men were sent out to find work for themselves, while the others staid and began to clear the ground and get ready to build.

Those who were sent away returned in the spring, each bringing his earnings with him, for they hold everything in common. The houses built by the Rappites are still standing, monuments of their German architecture. They are old and quaint-looking, with pointed gables and square windows, and many of them have deep arched cellars, resembling a dungeon more than a cellar. On a high hill close to the town and overlooking the country for miles, Rapp had an arched seat cut in the solid stone where he used to sit and watch the men at work, seeing that every one did his duty. It is a nice place, and on warm summer days it was much pleasanter for him to sit there smoking his long German pipe than to toil in the hot sun. Brother Sigler thinks he didn't smoke, but I am quite positive on this point.

We also visited the graveyard, which is enclosed by a wall of nicely dressed sandstone, each stone being about two feet long, one foot high, and sixteen inches in width. The wall is five feet high, surmounted by a coping of dressed stone, and at intervals of twenty feet, are little turrets. The entrance is through an arched stone gateway over which are inscriptions on a marble tablet, stating that here repose the remains of one hundred members of the Harmony community who died between the years 1805 and 1815, and passages from the Bible in reference to the resurrection. The gate is made of one solid stone, set on a pivot, and is six feet wide and about seven feet high. Inside the inclosure there is not the least sign of a grave or a gravestone; simply a level grass plat. I suppose this is to indicate that "Death levels all, both great and small," as the old primers used to have it. In 1815 they sold their landed interests and moved to Indiana and founded New Harmony, on the Wabash. They were not successful there, and after nine years they returned to Pennsylvania, and located and built Economy. The community now numbers about one hundred. They are estimated to be worth many millions.

Their old church at Harmony is still standing. They reserved it when they sold their other property, and subsequently gave it to the German Reformed congregation gratuitously. They are moral, live a life of celibacy and profess to learn more of and follow Jesus.

On Friday morning, in company with Brother Sigler and several young ladies and gentlemen, we came across the country to New Brighton, where we were to take the cars. It was the roughest road I have ever traveled. I don't believe you could find a worse one if you were to go out rough-road hunting. Your correspondent held the lines, and as we didn't want to miss the train, like Jehu, he "drove furiously," giving all a good "shaking up." In the afternoon we came to Wooster, where Brother Cassel met us. He and Brother John Willaman took us to Smithville, where we staid all night with our good Brother Willaman, where Elder Sigler preached, and where we saw a number of old friends.

The church at Wooster is now in a prosperous condition, and is under the pastoral care of Elder Cassel, who is well liked by the people. They enjoyed a precious work of grace last winter, and have added some sixty to the membership. The Sunday-school has largely increased, and this interest is also excellent. They have recently repainted and fixed up the house of worship, so that it presents a pleasant and attractive appearance. This is a good point for work, and the Ohio Eldership should give Wooster some special care. I met several of the brethren, and very much enjoyed my brief visit. Just as I was about leaving I had the pleasure of meeting Elder Geo. Wilson, who, though in advanced years, bears his age well and has a mind as vigorous as in former years.

At Wooster I joined three of our excursionists from Lebanon, and several from Cumberland county, and we came through safely to this city, reaching here yesterday morning at six o'clock.

Henceforth I become an integral part of the great excursion, which numbers over three hundred persons, and I shall hereafter write of *our* experiences by the way.

Here our excursion really only begins. We leave to-morrow at ten o'clock, *via* Chicago and Northwestern railroad in a special train. Chicago and the excursion will be reserved for a future letter.

NUMBER TWO.

CHICAGO—ROBERT COLLYER—THE STOCK YARDS—PACKING ESTABLISHMENTS—STARTING—OMAHA TO OGDEN— RECEPTION—SPEECHES.

SALT LAKE, JUNE 2, 1879.

My last letter was from Chicago. I said that I had become a part of the great Pacific Institute Excursion, the members of which gathered at the Palmer House, like segments of many family circles, and shall be known hereafter as that great composite, the P. I. E.

Sunday was one of Chicago's rainy days, but still a party of us went to hear Robert Collyer. His sermon was from Gen. xxxi:38. "This twenty years have I been with thee." It was an anniversary sermon, telling of his advent among them twenty years ago, and how they had grown during those years. He said they believed in God; in Jesus, his son, who came to reveal the Father's purposes; faith in man—in the power of God to reveal himself to man; faith in the Bible; in eternal life, and in the life like that set forth in the sermon on the mount. He is a pleasant speaker, and brings much of his old Methodist unction with him into the pulpit, a fact to which he referred in the sermon. We had hoped to see some of the Sunday-schools, as well as to hear some of Chicago's famous orthodox preachers, but were prevented by the rain and other circumstances.

I shall not attempt to describe the early history of Chicago, from its first permanent settlement in 1804; its incorporation into a city in 1837, and its subsequent growth and rapid development; its great fire in 1871, and again in 1874. With these your readers are already familiar. We visited the stock yards and other points of interest on Monday. The stock yards and pork packing establishment are truly wonders. The amount of land controlled by the company is 345 acres, of which the yards and pens occupy nearly

200 acres. The hotel and its grounds occupy 45 acres more. The capacity of the yards is more than 25,000 head of cattle, 100,000 hogs, and 22,000 sheep, besides stalls for more than 500 horses. There are more than thirty-two miles of under drainage, eight miles of streets and alleys, four miles of water troughs, and ten miles of feeding troughs. The place is a city in itself, and has a post office, bank, churches, schools, telegraph office, etc. The yards connect with all the railroads leading into the city. Everything seems confusion, but is regulated with the utmost care and precision.

The packing house is a wonder. It has a capacity for slaughtering 12,000 hogs daily. At the time of our visit they were killing only 3,000 daily. The hogs are driven into pens on the third story, and come out at the basement salted pork, packed, ready for the market. They are railroaded through the establishment as rapidly as bills are put through the Pennsylvania Legislature. The hogs are swung up by the legs, passed to the "sticker," who stands in a pool of blood; thence run to the scalding trough, dropped in, passed through it, and on to the revolving scraper, which removes the hair in twelve seconds; thence put through the hands of the finishers, who remove all the remaining hair; then swung up, disemboweled, beheaded, and shoved along, until they are divided, sent to the chill room, where they remain twenty-four hours, after which they are cut up into hams, shoulders, sides, etc., dropped again to the lower floor, where it is salted and stacked, ready for the packers. We timed one hog and were astonished to find that in six minutes from the time it left the sticker it was lying on the table with the bristles removed. In six seconds it was disemboweled. It is truly astonishing with what rapidity the work is done. The meat is shipped over the world, and is prepared to suit special markets; hams for London being trimmed in a particular manner to suit the English customers.

There were other points of interest visited, as the Water Works, Lincoln Park, and the various drives, with a description of which I will not worry your readers.

On Tuesday morning, now made famous in the lives of many, nearly three hundred tourists gathered at the depot of the Chicago and Northwestern railroad, where a special train of nine Pullman cars and one day coach, including baggage cars, was in waiting. A little after ten o'clock "all aboard" was shouted, and our train sped westward at the rate of over thirty miles an hour. We passed through the great and fertile State of Illinois, crossed the Mississippi, and by evening reached Cedar Rapids, Iowa, where the city turned out, with brass band, to give us a cordial reception. The next morning we reached Council Bluffs, where several hours were consumed in re-checking and weighing baggage, exchanging our tickets for those of the Union Pacific and making final preparations for the journey.

The Chicago and Northwestern railroad is one of the most direct routes from Chicago to Omaha. The road bed is smooth, stone ballast, and the management the very best. It passes through the most fertile part of Illinois and Iowa, as is evidenced by the splendidly cultivated farms, the large towns, and the excellent buildings. We have never gone over a better road. Our train made special time and reached Council Bluffs several hours in advance of the time

At Council Bluffs we were detained half a day by the Union Pacific railroad. The Union Pacific has a monopoly of the railroad business "across the continent," and does just as it pleases. When will Congress help the competing road, as it did this? It should certainly do so, for the interests of trade and travel demand it.

A few of us were enabled to cross the Missouri in advance of the excursion train, and spend several hours in Omaha. Omaha claims a population of 23,000, and there is considerable rivalry between it and Council Bluffs. We were fortunate enough to fall into the hands of the "local" of the *News*, to whom we are obliged for seeing much more of the city than we otherwise would have. The United States government has a fine building in which are the post office, the court room, and the various government offices. The school buildings, like those of other western towns, are very handsome, and from the grounds and observatory of the high school building you get a fine view of the city and the surrounding country. The mayor, whom all found to be most gentlemanly, and other dignitaries, were down when our excursion train arrived, and gave us an informal reception. On our train we find a number of prominent men, and are here joined by Dr. Vincent and Joseph Cook.

After a tiresome delay we are off, and our next two days will be spent on wheels. After leaving Omaha, the company in each car was requested to appoint one of their number as their representative, and thus a committee was constituted to attend to all the details of the excursion.

The following persons compose that committee: Rev. J. H. Vincent, D.D., Chairman, Plainfield, N. J.; Rev. Geo. A. Peltz, D.D., Secretary, Jamestown, N. Y.; Stephen Partridge, Car 0, St. Louis, Mo.; Rev. W. W. Hammond, Car 1, Detroit, Mich.; S. C. Bever, Esq., Car 2, Cedar Rapids, Iowa; E. W. Page, Esq., Car 3, New York; Ed. S. Wagoner, Esq., Car 4, Mechanicsburg, Pa.; Rev. J. M. Linn, Car 5, Winnebago, Ill.; J. H. Redsecker, Car 6, Lebanon, Pa.; Nathaniel Hills, Esq., Day Car, Brighton, Ill.; Rev. Sheldon Jackson, D.D., Car 7. Denver, Col.; Rev L. H. Trowbridge, D.D., Car 8, Detroit, Mich.

A daily paper was also issued, edited by Rev. Dr. Trowbridge and your correspondent. It was a novel paper and published in a novel way. As we had no press and type, each edition was in manuscript, and was read in each car. It contained the news from the various cars, personal paragraphs of the Pacific pilgrims, telegraphic, congressional, and general news, contributions, original poetry, and advertisements of lost and found.

The following is the name and style of the paper:

THE PACIFIC EXCURSIONIST.

PUBLISHED DAILY ON THE P. I. E. TRAIN.

MOTTO: For here we have no continuing city. Heb. 13:14.

THURSDAY, MAY 29, 1879.

A choir was also organized, under the leadership of Rev. George A. Ford, of Ramapo, N. Y., and furnished us with excellent singing. Morning and evening services were held in each car, addresses were delivered, and lessons drawn from Bible journeys.

We are now in Nebraska. The first view of the Platte Valley is an impressive one. Stretching away for miles and miles, as far as the eye can reach, is a treeless, trackless plain, smooth and green as a well-kept lawn. The Platte river is a fine, broad stream, but treacherous, we are told, as it is beautiful. It is of very shallow depth, and yet let a stranger attempt to cross it and he is apt to get into difficulty among its dangerous sands. Our train hurries along, but still the plains are before and around us, and when night comes on we are attracted by a prairie fire. It is impossible to describe it. Away off, miles from us, the flames spread out, increasing as they go, while large columns of smoke ascend heavenward. It was a most beautiful sight. Ranches, and towns of magnificent distances and great expectations, are all unconsciously passed, and morning still finds us on the prairie—at Sidney, a town of importance, and where we take breakfast. Sidney is the county seat of Cheyenne county, and contains about 1,500 people. From this point the stages start out for the Black Hills, and here the pioneer can purchase everything he wants in the way of supplies for the Hills. The distance to the Black Hills is 270 miles, and a daily stage takes passengers to Deadwood for $50 in winter, and less in summer. At this point the excursionists were delightfully entertained with a few songs by the Hutchinson Family.

From Sidney to Cheyenne, the next town of importance, is 102 miles. We have been gradually ascending, and at Cheyenne are 6,014 feet above the sea level. The town claims a population of 6,000 people. Their paper had an editorial cordially welcoming the tourists, and the people were out in holiday attire to greet us. As our train stopped quite a while, we had an opportunity of seeing a portion of the town. Rude frame houses are giving way to fine brick buildings, lawlessness has been stamped out, and quiet and order now reign supreme. We here learn how deceptive the distances are. The fort, which some of our party supposed to be a mile away, was actually three miles distant. At Sherman we are on the summit of the mountain, 8,242 feet above the sea. Here two of our engines are detached, and we are left with one to speed down the other side. When we awoke the next morning the ground was covered with snow, and the feathery flakes were still coming down gently.

One of our poets thus describes the scene:

> "This morning we have the beautiful snow,
> Coming down gently as onward we go,
> Covering the car tops and covering the trees,
> And causing us all to shiver and freeze.
> And would you believe it, the telegraph posts
> Looked in at the windows, 'like tall sheeted ghosts!'"

We are now in the Rocky Mountains, and away off sixty miles in the distance is Long's Peak, plainly visible, its summit capped with snow. At Rock Springs, a small watering station in the mountains, where many of the houses are built in the side of the hill and roofed with dirt, we had one of the most beautiful receptions on the road. They came, not with brass band and speeches, but a little Sunday-school, which gathers in this mountain village, came with banners to meet us, extending a hearty welcome "to our eastern friends." Several of our distinguished gentlemen were presented with bouquets of beautiful mountain flowers. At Evanston we are joined by a committee of citizens from Ogden, and thence our way to this place is through some of the grandest scenery on the route. The mountains are thousands of feet in height, and our train bowls along at the rate of thirty miles an hour, passing Castle Rock, a long line of sandstone bluffs which are worn by wind and rain until they have the appearance of old feudal castles. We are now in Echo Canyon, made famous by the Mormons in 1859. A thousand feet above the bed of the canyon, can be seen the fortifications erected by the Mormons for the purpose of defending themselves against Johnson's army. We pass Devil's Slide, two parallel walls of perpendicular rock, from twenty-five to fifty feet in height, extending from the base to the top of the mountain. It is one of the most wonderful of rock formations. We saw nothing of the devil, for he wasn't there.

We sped past the thousand-mile tree, the only tree visible, and which stands just one thousand miles west of Omaha. Thence our train hurries us into a beautiful little valley in which is the town of Weber. Here we see the mystic letters, "Z. C. M. I.," which, in Mormon rendering, mean "Zion's Co-operative Mercantile Institution."

Devil's Gate is the next place of interest passed. Here the mountains rise almost perpendicular to an extreme height. The pass is very narrow and presents a wild appearance. Weber river is confined to a very narrow channel, and goes rushing, roaring and seething over the rocks below. The bridge is fifty feet above the stream. The lofty mountains, the rushing waters, and the grand weird scenery, are objects of interest to the traveler which will not soon be forgotten. We have been running down the mountain from Evanston, and at last enter Ogden, where we remain over night, and then go to Salt Lake City.

The people of Ogden were out *en masse* to give us a welcome. Large pavilions were erected and supper was waiting. Preceded by a brass band, the tourists were escorted to the pavilion, when Gov. Emery, on behalf of the people, extended a cordial welcome, as follows:

"*Ladies and Gentlemen*—On behalf of the people of Utah I extend to you a cordial greeting to our Territory. We are always pleased to meet our friends from the east to the west, and give them such advantages to witness our scenery, our civilization and our society as they may require. I understand that many of you go to California, attracted, no doubt, by the glowing accounts which you have read and heard of the splendid climate and the gorgeous scenery there. Permit me to state, ladies and gentlemen, that here in Utah we have scenery rivaling that of the famed Yosemite; we have attractions such as you must see to appreciate. And before going, I would advise that you enjoy a bath in the waters of the great Salt Lake. These waters contain some twenty-five per cent. of pure salt. After a brief encounter with the briny waves anyone is enabled to float upon them with but very little exertion. The water also contains enough soda to make a bath healthful and invigorating. A great deal has been said about the climate of California, but here, I venture to say, we have as fine a climate as you will find in the country. And I think we have finer skies than can be found elsewhere in the world, excepting Italy and Southern California. But I am sure you must be better prepared and will receive in a more welcome manner the repast now before you than anything in the way of speech-making. I again extend a hearty welcome." (Applause.)

At the conclusion of the Governor's address, Dr. Vincent replied in the following language:

"*Ladies and Gentlemen*—Permit me to express thanks as a representative of the Pacific excursionists, for the generous words of welcome we have heard and this repast which is before us. We come as citizens of the United States, loyal to our country and faithful to the ideas of Christianity inculcated by the Bible—the fountain of Christianity. Our object is and has been to further the cause of Sunday-schools in this country. We believe in preparing the minds of our youth by wholesome teachings, that they may have the advantages of correct, Christian-like principles to guide them in after life. We also desire to inculcate a sentiment of harmony and, I may say, entire catholicity throughout our dominions such as will lead to a better understanding and a more perfect union of ideas among those who aim at Christianity pure and simple. While faithful to our God we are faithful to the laws of our country, and are always pleased to meet with those who are in accord with us on those questions. I realize fully that most of our party, like myself, desire food for the body rather than food for the mind; therefore I will not prolong my remarks. I again thank you."

Mr. Joseph Stanford, representing Ogden city, then appeared and said:

"*Ladies and Gentlemen*—I very much regret, through indisposition and family affliction, the absence on this occasion of the mayor, the Hon. Lester J. Herrick. At the same time, I feel much gratified in the honor conferred in extending to you in his behalf, and in behalf of the members of the common council of Ogden city, a cordial and hearty welcome.

"Our young, yet growing and prosperous city, containing only about 8,000 inhabitants, may not possess for you so many charms or so much to draw forth expressions of praise and admiration as those much older and more populous cities of the east through which you have passed *en route* to these mountain fastnesses. We have no public buildings or edifices exhibiting much if any display of architectural design or skilled artistic and mechanical ability. No public parks, museums and a hundred other institutions of profit and amusement peculiar to cities in the east. Our adornments and places of interest are those only which nature has provided—our broad and fertile valleys, our canyons, our mountain passes, our lakes, rivers and springs, the latter of varied temperatures of heat and mineral properties. We must, however, with due and becoming modesty, claim that our city possesses all the elements, facilities and surroundings, necessary to constitute her in time a great commercial centre.

"Ogden is the junction city of the great highway across the continent—the Atlantic and Pacific railroads, also of the Utah Central and Southern and the Utah and Northern railroads. Although our city is small, we claim that its inhabitants are an industrious, healthy, peaceful, happy and consequently a prosperous people, and we trust you will find your brief sojourn in our midst to be both pleasant and profitable; and notwithstanding the controlling influence is directly or indirectly exercised by the old settlers or the dominant party, generally designated as "Mormons," you will find liberty, freedom and protection extended to all creeds, classes and professions. And gentlemen, as you are particularly interested in the religious, moral and intellectual welfare of the rising generation, I am happy to be in a position to state that Ogden is not lacking in her duty in these important matters, for besides her ten day-schools, there are seven Sabbath-schools, with an average attendance of eight hundred scholars.

"We further hope that your visit among us will be made a source of information and profit, not only as regards our mineral, commercial and agricultural interests and prospects, but that our political, social and moral status may be correctly understood, and represented by you when you shall have passed from our midst. I again, ladies and gentlemen, extend to you, one and all, a most hearty and cordial welcome." (Applause.)

Dr. Peltz then came forward and responded, as follows:

"*Ladies and Gentlemen*—I return you our sincere thanks for the kind words which have been spoken and the cordial reception given us. We are glad for the showing you make in your secular and religious schools. You have spoken of the absence of public buildings or edifices displaying architectural design, or artistic ability; but God has put around your city some of his most beautiful works. God's grandeur in nature is excelled only by his grandeur in character. As Sunday-school teachers we are laboring to put grandeur into the character and lives of those whom we are teaching. I again thank you for your generous welcome, and may God bless you."

The delegates were then invited to be seated, and were served with an excellent supper, prepared by Messrs. Keeney & Ziegler, proprietors of the Keeney House. They are from Cumberland county, Pa., and keep an excellent hotel. The supper was in the interest of one of the local churches.

The next morning a number of the tourists went to see Ogden Canyon, while the majority left on the train for Salt Lake City.

ACROSS THE CONTINENT. 19

Ogden Canyon is worth a visit. The Ogden river forms a series of cascades and falls; the scenery is wild; the walls of the canyon are hundreds of feet in height; and the sulphur and hot springs are wonders in nature.

We returned from the canyon in time to catch the afternoon train for Salt Lake City, which we reach in the evening, and will attempt to describe in a future letter.

NUMBER THREE.

SALT LAKE CITY—MORMON SUNDAY-SCHOOL—THE TABERNACLE—JOSEPH SMITH—MORMON RELIGION.

SAN FRANCISCO, JUNE 16, 1879.

The approach to Salt Lake City is through a delightful country. A few miles from Ogden we catch a view of the great Salt Lake, shining like a mirror in the afternoon sun. On our left are high towering mountains, their summits capped with snow, while in the valley are the homes of the Mormon farmers who are busy cultivating the soil. Within a few miles of the city we pass the Hot Springs, and the train stops so that we may have an opportunity of stepping off and seeing them. The water pours out from the hill in a large stream, and is so hot that an egg can be boiled in it in a few minutes. It is strongly sulphurous, and leaves a permanent stain on white garments.

Salt Lake City is one of the most beautiful cities it has been our privilege to see, and contains a population of about 20,000, three-fourths of whom are Mormons. It was our good fortune to stop at the Continental Hotel, formerly kept by a Mormon, but now managed by G. L. Erb, a Lancaster county Dutchman, who also runs the Walker House. They are the finest hotels in the city. The

Continental has a fine veranda, and is surrounded by beautiful trees, making it a most delightful place.

The streets of Salt Lake City are each one hundred feet wide, the pavements sixteen feet, making the streets, from house to house, 132 feet wide. The houses outside the business centres are surrounded by large yards, filled with trees, shrubbery and flowers. At the time of our visit (June 1st), the roses were in full bloom, and added greatly to the beauty of the place.

The city is irrigated, the water for this purpose being brought from a canyon some three miles distant and conveyed throughout the city in ditches. The crystal flood pours down the sides of the streets, and is as clean and pure as when it leaves its home in the mountains. Arrangements are made for running the water into the yards, and is regulated by law, so that each inhabitant may have his proportionate share. The water for drinking and other purposes is brought from the same canyon, and is of most excellent quality. Whatever Brigham Young may have been, and however much we may condemn him for his polygamous views, he certainly deserves great credit for making this barren wilderness bloom and blossom as the rose.

Of course, in Salt Lake City, the great thing to see is the Mormon worship, and so we spent Sunday in seeing this as thoroughly as we could.

The *Deseret News*, the Mormon daily, in its Saturday's issue gave a cordial welcome to the excursionists, and the people generally were exceedingly clever and communicative.

The city is divided into twenty-one wards, each presided over by a bishop. In each ward there is a school-house, in which morning and evening services and Sunday-school is held. In the afternoon service is held in the tabernacle where they all congregate.

At the ward school which we attended, the services were opened by singing a song of welcome, for there were a number of tourists present. The bishop led in prayer, and prayed for the strangers in the gates, that they might comprehend the light by which they were surrounded. The minutes of the previous session were read and approved, the children as well as the adults having the right to vote. The school was then formally opened, the different classes directed what was to be studied, when the smaller children withdrew to one of the side rooms, the intermediate class to another, and the advanced class remaining. By special invitation, Rev. Dr. Trowbridge and your correspondent addressed the children. After the study of the lesson the schools assembled in the main room where all partook of the communion. Water, however, is used instead of wine, and the smallest child as well as the gray haired sire partakes of it. After this they desired to hear from the tourists, when several short speeches were made by some of the persons present.

In the afternoon, worship was held in the great tabernacle which will hold, they claim, 14,000 persons. It is 250 feet long by 150 wide. The roof is supported by forty-six columns of cut sandstone, the spaces between them being used for windows and doorways. From these walls the roof springs in an unbroken arch, forming, it is said, the largest self-sustaining roof on the continent, except the Grand Union Depot in New York. The ceiling of the roof is sixty-five feet from the floor. The ceiling was festooned with evergreens, while a large chandelier of evergreens and artificial flowers was suspended from the ceiling. The organ, which is in the rear of the pulpit, is one of the largest in the country, and was built by themselves. There are three pulpits immediately in the rear of, and raised from two to three feet above each other. The choir is seated in the rear of the pulpits, and below and around the pulpits are the seats for the dignitaries of the church. The singing is splendid, the choir being composed of probably seventy-five males and females, with a leader who seems to thoroughly understand his business.

The bread and water are passed around by the deacons, who proceed noislessly, during which time is the preaching. We had four addresses delivered with much earnestness, and intended specially for the Gentiles. It was the merest trash, presented with a great deal of seeming earnestness, each speaker taking his cue from the first, and giving us the same stuff in a different form. Reserved seats had been provided for the excursionists, and so we had a good opportunity of seeing and observing. We did not see one handsome female among all the Mormon women. There are some intelligent looking men and women among them, but the majority of women look degraded, and devoid of intelligence; and the same applies to the hard laboring class of men. There were fully 8,000 persons present in the tabernacle, as it was *the* service of the day.

Brigham Young owned a vast estate. His property covers entire blocks in the most eligible portion of the city, showing that while he took care of Zion, he had an eye to his own interests. Amelia Palace, a magnificent residence commenced by Brigham for Amelia, his favorite wife, is not yet completed. When finished it will be occupied by President Taylor, as Amelia is building herself a smaller residence.

Within three miles of the city is Camp Douglass, where are stationed some of the U. S. troops, and from which point you have a fine view of the city and surrounding country. Salt Lake City does a large business, being a point from which many towns and stations in the surrounding Territories get their supplies. "Zion's Co-operative Mercantile Institution," organized in 1868, occupies the largest building in the city and carries goods of all descriptions. Through the kindness of the managing editor of their Sunday-school publications we were shown through the establishment. The building cost $175,000. Walker Bros. have the largest Gentile establishment in the city and do a large business. The annual sales of these two establishments, we are informed, exceed $5,000,000 a year.

On Sunday evening we had the pleasure of meeting Mr. Johnson, who came over with Brigham Young in 1847, and is one of the oldest members of the Church. He met a number of us for a friendly interchange of views, and to answer such questions as we might wish to ask. He told us that when Joseph Smith was between fourteen and fifteen years of age he professed religion at a revival meeting in Ontario county, N. Y. There was great quarreling among the different churches as to which should get the converts, and this gave him great distraction of mind. He went into the woods to pray, asking God to teach him the true religion. The heavens were opened and two personages stood before him, and one pointing to the other said, "This is my beloved son, hear ye him." He was told the religious societies were all teaching incorrect doctrines, and he must join none of them. On the night of the 21st of September, 1823, the angel Moroni appeared to him three times, and told him that there was a record written on gold plates giving an account of the ancient inhabitants of America and God's dealing with them, deposited in a particular place in the earth. With the record were two stones set in silver bows, called the Urim and Thummin, by which he would be enabled to translate the writing on the plates. The angel directed him to tell his father, who advised him to obey the direction, as it was from God. He accordingly went to the place, and, with a crowbar, pried off the stone, saw the plates, but by some indiscreetness on his part he was not permitted to touch them. After four years, spent in prayer, the angel told him he could get the plates. On the 22d of September, 1827, they were placed in his hands. They were written in the Reformed Egyptian, a language not known to the earth; but by the use of the Urim and Thummin Joseph was enabled to make a translation of that portion which was unsealed. The translation was published in 1830, and called the Book of Mormon. The plates, which after the translation were returned to the angel, were about eight inches long, seven inches wide, and a little thinner than ordinary tin.

On the 6th of April, 1830, the first church was organized, with six members. A year after, they settled in Ohio, and the same year moved to Independence, Mo., from which place they were driven in 1833, and in 1839 they settled and built Nauvoo, Ill., from whence they were driven in 1846, and made their journey overland to the present city of Salt Lake.

This is the Mormon side. Let us now look at the facts from the other side. The Rev. Solomon Spaulding, who graduated at Dartmouth College in 1785, moved to Ohio early in the present century.

He gathered from legends and traditions a quantity of material and wrote a story, after the manner of Bible stories. This was taken to Pittsburg to be printed; the copy was surreptitiously stolen by Sidney Rigdon, and, passing into the hands of Joseph Smith, was used by him and a few others for the purpose of playing upon the credulity of the people. It was passed off as a new revelation from heaven, and called the Book of Mormon. It pretends to give an account of two tribes of Jews—the Jaredites, who went westward after the building of the Tower of Babel. The Indians of North America are the descendants of these tribes, according to the Book of Mormon. Mr. Johnson did not tell us that Smith and Rigdon ran away from Ohio to escape the officers of the law. He failed also to tell us that they confiscated the property of their neighbors in Missouri and Illinois, and appropriated it to their own use, and for this the people rose up against them and drove them out. These things were forgotten when he gave us a history of Mormonism.

The Mormon Church believes in the Bible and the Book of Mormon. It believes in the trinity as three distinct persons. It has four ordinances: Faith in Christ, repentance, baptism by immersion and for remission of sin, and laying on of hands for the gift of the Holy Ghost. They believe that Jesus will return to earth and establish a New Jerusalem in Jackson county, Missouri. As, according to their faith, Christ is going to reign on the earth, they, therefore, are endeavoring to make their places as handsome as possible, and build temples for him. They are now erecting a new temple which will cost several millions of dollars.

Aside from their loathsome polygamy, which is a blot on our civilization, and degrading especially to the women, they are quite a pleasant people, and treated us with very great consideration.

There are quite a number of apostate Mormons in Salt Lake City. They have withdrawn from the Church, and those who had more than one wife have provided for the support of the others and their children, and are living now with but one, and she the lawful one.

Services were held in the Protestant churches. Dr. Vincent preached in the morning, and Joseph Cook lectured in the evening.

He gave a prelude on Mormonism, in which he tore the mask from their system, and exposed it in all its loathsomeness. He gave Mormonism a terrible excoriation, and set the leaders and editors howling and cursing, and delighted the Gentiles, who are exposed to much persecution and who could not live there were it not for the power of the Federal arm.

But my letter has already grown too long. Our journey westward, from Salt Lake, and the Yosemite, will be sent later.

NUMBER FOUR.

SALT LAKE TO OGDEN—ELKO—WINNEMUCCA—HUMBOLDT— TRUCKEE—SACRAMENTO—MADERA—BERRY TESTIMONIAL—SOUVENIER.

SAN FRANCISCO, JUNE 17, 1879.

We left Salt Lake City on Monday afternoon and Ogden the same evening. At the latter place we took the cars of the Central Pacific railroad for California, the Union Pacific terminating at Ogden. The road runs along Salt Lake for some distance giving us a good view of this great inland sea. When we awoke the next morning we were in the State of Nevada, two hundred miles west of Ogden. We were delayed during the night by a freight train, so that we did not reach Elko, the breakfast station, until nearly noon. Need I say we were hungry?

Elko is the county seat of Elko county, and has a population, it is said, of 1,200. Of course it is a city. What in the east is called a village, is here a city. It was Bayard Taylor, I believe, who aptly said, that in the west they drive down a stake, mark out a street, and call the place a city. Elko City, then,—for we must conform to the habits of the country—does not present many attractions for the tourist. It may have some fine public buildings and private residences, but we failed to see them. The State University, costing $30,000, is located here, but we did not see the buildings. The city, however, has a *very* unpretentious appearance, and leads one to believe that it is yet in its swaddling clothes.

There were quite a number of the Shoshone Indians at the station. Some of them, men and women, were sitting on the ground around a blanket playing cards for money. They are great gamblers, I am told. I presume they are civilized. They are a squalid looking lot of individuals, and you would have to draw on your imagination immensely, if you were to work yourself into any sort of enthusiasm over these "noble red men of the forest." Poor Lo! He needs to be honestly dealt with by the government, whose ward he is, taught some industrial occupation, missionaries to teach him the gospel, and in addition to all these, plenty of good soap and water.

We now have the Humboldt river and mountains in sight, and the scenery is varied and beautiful. Palisade is a station in the mountains, and the junction of the Eureka and Palisade railroad. You can see large quantities of base bullion pigs piled up at the station awaiting shipment. It is brought from the Eureka smelting works. Over 38,000,000 pounds of crude bullion was transported over the road during the year 1878.

When we reached Battle Mountain we found a Sunday-school drawn up in line—not of battle but of greeting—in front of the station. They greeted us with a song, after which Dr. Vincent addressed them. Sunday-school papers and tracts were distributed, the engine's shrill whistle shrieked a chorus, and we mounted the cars and were off.

In the afternoon we stopped at Winnemucca. The citizens were out *en masse* and gave us a grand reception. A brass band discoursed some excellent music, after which Rev. J. R. Berry, our master of transportation, was called on for a speech. He thanked them for the reception, and after a few pleasant words of greeting, introduced Dr. Vincent. He spoke of the reception, and of the excursion, and said it was the purpose of the Sunday-school to train the boys and girls to love whatsoever things are pure, honest, just and true, and to trample under foot, with righteous vengeance whatever is low, and base and sinful. He said he did not want to make a speech. There was a gentleman present whom he wanted them to hear. He was an excellent man. The only bad thing about him is, he is a Baptist. He introduced Rev. Dr. Peltz, amid the prolonged cheers of the people.

Dr. Peltz said he was pleased to meet them. During the war for the suppression of the rebellion we had two kinds of forces,—the army which fought on the land, and the navy which fought on the water. Both branches of the service did well, each contributing its share toward the grand result, and both fighting under the same old flag. Now, he said, my friend Dr. Vincent belongs to the army, the land forces, and I belong to the navy, but we are both fighting for the same end and under the same flag,—the banner of our Lord Jesus Christ.

At the conclusion of Dr. Peltz's remarks, Judge Berry, of Winnemucca, was called out. He said a few words congratulatory of the excursion, and the pleasure they always felt in meeting friends from the east.

The reception was a most enjoyable affair, and at its conclusion our train moved off to the musical strains of the band.

Forty miles from Winnemucca we come to Humboldt, on the edge of the great desert of Nevada. Everything has a look of utter desolation, except at the station. Here all is bright and green and cheerful looking. In front of the hotel is a fountain, while the trees and grass have a peculiar freshness. We stopped here about an hour and had supper, after which Mr. Cook gave us a short speech. He is an intellectual giant, and when he speaks you are sure to learn something. He told us of the greatness of our country; of the vast extent of territory comprising it; of the millions it was capable of furnishing with homes and food; and of the tremendous stretch from its eastern to its most western limit, so that San Francisco is really about midway between the two. He was roundly applauded at the close of his remarks.

Humboldt demonstrates the fact that these plains can be made productive by irrigation. Thirty miles north of the station are sulphur mines which produce sulphur in a nearly pure state. The specimens which I secured are very fine. It is brought to the railroad in wagons, and thence shipped to San Francisco where it is refined and sent to the markets of the world.

Our route now lay across this alkali desert. The air is hot. We are obliged to keep windows and doors closed, and even then the fine dry sand sifted in through the crevices, rendering travel exceedingly unpleasant, and the cars stifling. One young lady in our car gasped for breath, called for water, and declared she would die before morning. "She couldn't live through it. She would suffocate." She didn't suffocate. She didn't die. The next day when we were over the plains she had forgotten all about it, and was as gay as usual.

When we awoke the next morning we were among the Sierra Nevada mountains, and they really are mountains, from 6,000 to 10,000 feet high. Between this and Sacramento we pass through some of the finest scenery along the route. Our road runs along the Truckee river which has some rapids as fine as you will see anywhere. I think they are fully as magnificent as those above the Whirlpool at Niagara, but of course there is not the volume of water. The morning is cool, the air bracing, and we find overcoats and wraps none too heavy.

We soon reach Truckee, where we stop. It is not much of a—city,—I almost forgot,—but in its early days enjoyed an unenviable reputation. A gentleman familiar with its early history told us that in early times many a man was buried here with his boots on, having been killed over the gaming table, and carried away and buried without further ceremony. The principal street is near the railroad, and of the three dozen houses, nineteen I think are drinking saloons.

After leaving Truckee we begin the ascent of the mountain. Before reaching the summit we pass over the "mule-shoe," a curve which for extent surpasses the famous horse-shoe curve on the

Pennsylvania railroad. We also pass through miles of snow-sheds, and catch a glimpse of Donner Lake, a splendid sheet of water in which the high mountains are beautifully photographed. The old emigrant road used to lead along this lake. It was here that Mr. Donner and some of his party perished in the winter of 1846. They were snowed up and their cattle stampeded. When the emigrants were found the following spring, they were dead. A German who was with them was found alive, was crazy, and had eaten a portion of the dead bodies of Mr. and Mrs. Donner. He was cared for, and when reason returned he was accused of having killed them. He stoutly protested his innocence. The matter remains a mystery.

But our train has been going on while we have stopped to talk about the Donner Lake mystery. We reach the summit, and stop in the snow shed. Some of the party have a most delightful time snow-balling each other on the 4th of June. There is a hotel on the summit, and in a box, covered with a cloth, was quite an ornithological curiosity,—a red bat weighing two pounds. Many whose curiosity was excited raised the cover only to see a brick-bat suspended by a cord. They retired amid the audible smiles of those who had been there before.

We now begin the descent of the mountain and pass a number of places with classical names, as Dutch Flat, You Bet, Red Dog, and the like, and reach Gold Run, a mining town, where we got our first sight of hydraulic mining. The water is brought for miles in flumes along the mountain side and over chasms, and forced through pipes against the sides of the mountains. The gravel and stones are washed away and passing through sluices is held long enough so as to permit the gold to settle, which is then collected. Near Gold Run the top of the mountain is entirely washed away.

We have seen magnificent scenery at various points along the route, but Cape Horn, which we now approach, surpasses everything we have before seen. Before reaching it we catch a glimpse, on our left, of the American river, foaming and rushing along in a narrow mountain-gorge, nearly two thousand feet below us. Our train rushes along while every eye is strained to take in all the scenery. At last we reach Cape Horn, and the train stops. It is perfectly sublime! On our right the mountain rises almost vertically for thousands of feet, while on our left is an almost perpendicular descent of twenty-five hundred feet. We look up to the mountain top almost reaching to cloud-land, and then down, down, into the little valley, and see the river, like a thread of silver, dashing along over its rocky bed; the trees become diminutive shrubs, and the people in the fields below as mere human specks on the surface. It is the grandest view on the whole route. "All aboard" rings along the line, and we are brought to realize that we are not in wonderland, and must get aboard if we want to continue the excursion.

We bound down the mountain, reach Colfax, and after stopping long enough to dine, start for Sacramento, which we reach about three o'clock.

Need I tell you Sacramento is the capital of the State; that it is built on the Sacramento river; that it contains thousands of people; that it is a place of very considerable business enterprise; that it has been burnt out, and washed out several times, and each time has risen like a Phœnix and put on new strength? You know these things. You know, too, that in order to guard against a flood, after they found levees would not do, they have raised the city. So I'll not stop to tell you anything of its history. We have pleasant recollections of Sacramento, for didn't the good Sunday-school people meet us at the train; didn't they take us to the State House in carriages, omnibuses and street cars, and didn't they give us a splendid reception? Of course they did, and we say, God bless the Sunday-school people of Sacramento.

It was a most enjoyable affair. The reception was held in the Senate Chamber. As we entered we were presented with handsome bouquets. After we were seated, the pupils of the high-school sang a song of greeting, and then Rev. Dr. Bentley and Secretary-of-State Beck made addresses of welcome, to which Rev. Dr. Vincent and Rev. Joseph Cook responded. Then we partook of refreshments furnished by the ladies of the city, and had more bouquets presented us as we left. We shall not forget Sacramento!

Many of our tourists left us here, going direct to San Francisco *via* Vallejo, while about two hundred of us continued our journey toward Stockton, where some got off to take the Big Oak Flat route into the valley. The rest of us went to Lathrop, and thence to Merced, where we again dropped a number of cars and passengers, so that they might go into the valley by the Merced and Coulterville routes. The remainder went on to Madera, which we reached sometime in the night, and where we lay until morning, and were then waked to take the stages into the Yosemite.

Our journey, thus far, had been most pleasant, and we felt it was due the Rev. J. R. Berry, our Master of Transportation, who had arranged for our trip Across the Continent, to make some suitable acknowledgment of our appreciation. The matter was presented to the tourists, who contributed liberally. The Executive Committee, at a meeting, appointed Revs. Drs. Vincent, Jackson and Peltz a committee to purchase the testimonial.

It was also ordered that a Souvenier of the excursion be prepared and published, taking the letters of Dr. Peltz, and some of the articles from *The Pacific Excursionist*, with the addresses of all the tourists. The editors of the paper, and Dr. Peltz, were appointed a committee to prepare it, and several hundred copies were subscribed for. Thus ended our excursion by rail.

Our trip into the Yosemite Valley by stage will be described in our next.

NOTE.—A handsome gold watch and chain were subsequently purchased and presented to Mr. Berry. It bears the inscription: "Presented to Rev. J. R. Berry by the Members of the P. I. E., J. H. Vincent, Sheldon Jackson, Geo. A. Peltz, Committee."

NUMBER FIVE.

THE YOSEMITE VALLEY—THE ROUTES—THE ASSEMBLY—ADDRESSES.

SAN FRANCISCO, JUNE 20, 1879.

The Yosemite Valley is about 160 miles from San Francisco, in a direct line. It is 88 miles from the nearest railroad station. For the benefit of your readers, let me say there are five stage routes leading into the valley, on all of which good stages are run. Two roads lead in by Stockton, on one of which you can go by the Calaveras grove of big trees, making 148 miles of staging. By leaving out the Calaveras trees you have only 88 miles of staging, and pass through the Tuolumne grove. This is the shortest route into the valley, requiring but two days to reach San Francisco from the valley. The other routes are the Coulterville, which leaves Merced, passes through the Merced grove and has 88 miles of staging, requiring three days to reach San Francisco. The others are the Mariposa and Madera. The Mariposa starts from Merced, passes the Mariposa grant, within six miles of the Mariposa grove, and has 97 miles of staging. The Madera is a new route, starting from Madera, passes within six miles of the Fresno, and four miles of the Mariposa grove, and has 92 miles of staging. The latter roads bring you into the valley by Inspiration Point, from which you have a fine view of the valley. The best way is to go in by one and come out by the other, as each has its special advantages and attractions. The Calaveras trees are the highest and the grove the best kept, and are worthy of a visit. By any but the Stockton route you miss these.

We went by the Madera, having been told it was the best. There can certainly be no better. The grade is easy, the road bed smooth, the scenery grand, the coaches new and elegant, and the drivers round the curves and dash up and down the grades with a care and skill that is truly surprising. However, since we have been there we say, not being interested in any of the routes, go in by one and come out by the other. The fare, by stage, is about twenty-five dollars one way. If you buy a round-trip ticket you are obliged to come out by the same road you went in, and thus lose a different kind of scenery, unless you can make an exchange of tickets in the valley, as we did.

At six o'clock on Thursday morning, June 5th, the six-horse stage pulled up in front of the hotel. Sixteen passengers and baggage were quickly loaded, the driver cracked his whip, and we were off like a flying missile shot from a mortar. Jack rabbits with great long ears sit on their haunches and look at us in blank amazement as we hurry by. Grey squirrels that burrow in the ground scamper off quickly to some safe retreat, while by their holes sit the owls, blinking and staring at us in the wisest manner possible, as if they had read the papers and knew all about the excursion. We change horses six times before reaching Clark's, where we stop for the night, and are glad to take a "shake down," and sleep soundly.

The next morning we are off again for the valley, twenty-seven miles distant, which is reached shortly after noon.

We get the first view of the valley from Inspiration Point, and as its grandeur and beauty is unfolded, every voice is hushed. Yosemite, of which we had read and dreamed in our waking moments; Yosemite, with its towering crags and precipices, rearing their lofty summits heavenward nearly a mile; with its waterfalls nearly three thousand feet high, dashing and thundering in their fall,—lies spread out before us a vivid reality.

We look down three thousand feet, and see the Merced river winding along through the valley, while across the mighty chasm, by the side of El Capitan, the Virgin's Tears Falls, sparkling like a silver ribbon, dash down the side of the mountain upon the rocks below, and its waters are mingled with those of the river. El Capitan, like a guardian of the valley, stands before us in all its grandeur, its lofty summit seeming to reach the skies. To your right are the Cathedral rocks, by the side of which the Bridal Veil falls over the mountain. As all this bursts upon your view, you are impressed with the magnitude of Yosemite.

We had told our driver that we wanted to beat **Dr.** Vincent's stage into the Valley. We agreed to walk up the mountains, which we did, and we even promised to carry the mustangs if it were necessary, which we didn't, and here we were, the first to get a sight of it. But at Inspiration Point we are yet more than five miles from the hotels. So starting down the trail, the driver gave the horses the rein and we flew around the zigzag curves, until our hair stood on end; we held our breath, and held on to the seats, and at last assured him we were not in so much of a hurry after all. But Henry's blood was up, and he was not to be stopped by anything. Away flew the ponies, past the Bridal Veil Falls, past El Capitan, with its granite walls grey with time, and the Cathedral rocks pointing their spires to the very clouds, and brought us up in front of Black's hotel, where we had an opportunity of washing off the dust of travel, and sitting down quietly in front of the magnificent Yosemite Falls.

Who can describe Yosemite? We had read of it; we had seen pictures and imagined what it was like, but all of these give but the faintest idea of its grandeur. The valley is about nine miles long by about one and a half miles wide, through which flows the Merced river, a stream of clear, crystal water formed by the melting snows on the high Sierras. The walls of the valley are of grey granite, nearly vertical, and from 3,000 to 6,150 feet in height above the valley, while the valley is 4,100 feet above the level of the sea. Yosemite Fall, the highest in the valley, though not the largest body of water, is 2,634 feet high, the first fall which the water makes being 1,600 feet. You never tire of sitting and watching it as it plunges over the top of the mountain, sending up a noise like distant thunder, and continually changing its form as it is blown about by the wind. Bridal Veil is much smaller, and is only 940 feet high, but its thin, gossamer-like form, swayed by the air, produces an effect indescribably grand.

There are trails up all the mountain sides; and as you stand in the valley and look up you wonder how it is possible to scale the sides of these bare walls; but man's ingenuity put to the test has accomplished the difficult task, and you can ride to the top without the least fear, for the horses are well trained, and step as carefully as a man. You can walk up if you wish, but you will find it a hard climb, and feel the next day as one of the excursionists said he did, that you have a Sentinel Dome in one leg and a Glacier Point in the other. If you wish to ascend but one, the Glacier Point trail is the best, as you will get a finer and more extended view from this than from any other, except Cloud's Rest or South Dome, up the latter of which you have to work your way 700 feet by rope. From Glacier Point, 3,200 feet high, you ascend to Sentinel Dome, a thousand feet higher, and have a magnificent view of the mountains—Starr King, the Lyall group, Hoffman and others, stretching away as far as the eye can reach. Here, on the Dome, you may gather flowers with one hand, while with the other you gather snow. It is a day's work, but you feel amply repaid, for as you came up, at every turn of the zigzag path new features of the valley were opened before you, while men looked like the merest specks, fields seemed no larger than garden patches, and large trees like shrubs.

You will want to visit Mirror Lake early in the morning, before sunrise. The lake is not large, but is as transparent as glass, and reflects the mountains like a mirror. The sun rose at 8.40, and as he slowly climbed over the mountains, the view was indescribable. The mountain tops were fringed as if with gold, and their reflection in the lake was magnificent. We saw the waning moon reflected in the lake, go out before the rising sun. It was a sight such as we never beheld, and perhaps will never again.

When you are in the valley, don't fail to go to Snow's and see Vernal and Nevada Falls. They haven't the height of Yosemite, but to our mind this is the prettiest portion of the valley. Perhaps we saw it under more favorable circumstances. It is five miles from Black's, and the trail leads along the Merced which forms a series of magnificent cascades. The main body of the Merced flows over these two falls. The Nevada is six hundred feet high, four times as high as Niagara, and about sixty feet wide. The water is broken into fragments and falls on the rocks below with a deafening noise. The scenery is of the wildest and grandest. The Cap of Liberty, a stupendous mass of rock, isolated and nearly perpendicular on all sides, rises to nearly two thousand feet. Broderick stands just behind and is nearly or quite as high, while still farther back is Cloud's Rest and South Dome. The distance between Vernal and Nevada Falls is probably a half-mile, and the river, as it rushes madly on, forms some of the most magnificent rapids to be seen anywhere. Near the bridge the water is compelled to pass through a narrow granite trough and is broken into particles which are tossed into the air and glitter in the sunlight like diamonds. Farther on it is spread out like a lace curtain as it plunges over a large flat rock, changing its form every moment, and falls into a large basin where it is placid as a lake of glass, and gently flows to the top of Vernal Falls, when it takes its final plunge of four hundred feet onto the rocky bed below.

Snow will give you an excellent dinner for a dollar, entertain you hospitably, and make you feel at home. We saw on the register, under date of June 12, 1875, the names of our friends Geo. Smuller and his estimable daughter, with the remark that they were greatly pleased with the host and hostess. Mrs. Snow said she remembered them very well, as they spent several days there.

"It doesn't rain in California in summer," we were told. It does rain in the Yosemite, and it did at Snow's. So gathering some empty sacks, we put them over the ladies' shoulders, and started for the valley, which, when reached, a brisk canter soon brought us to the hotel, where the costumes of the ladies were greatly admired.

We give below the

TABLE OF ALTITUDES AT YOSEMITE VALLEY.

WATERFALLS.

Indian Name.	Signification.	American Name.	Height.
Po-ho-no	Spirit of the Evil Wind	Bridal Veil	940 feet
Yo-sem-ite	Large Grizzly Bear		2,634 feet

First Fall, 1,600 feet; Second Fall, 534 feet; Third Fall, 500 feet.

Indian Name.	Signification.	American Name.	Height.
Pi-wa-ack	Cataract of Diamonds	Vernal	350 feet
Yo-wi-ye	Meandering	Nevada	700 feet
To-lool-we-ack	Rushing Water	South Fork	500 feet
To-coy-æ	Shade to Indian Baby Basket	Royal Arch Fall	2,000 feet
Loya		Sentinel Fall	3,270 feet
Lung-oo-too-koo-ya	Long and Slender	Ribbon Fall	3,300 feet

MOUNTAINS.

Indian Name.	Signification.	American Name.	Height.
Tis-sa-ack	Goddess of the Valley	South Dome	5,000 feet
		Cloud's Rest	6,150 feet
To-coy-æ	Shade to Indian Baby Basket	North Dome	3,725 feet
		Glacier Point	3,200 feet
Hunto	The Watching Eye	Round Tower	2,400 feet
Mah-ta	Martyr Mountain	Cap of Liberty	3,100 feet
		Mt. Starr King	5,100 feet
Tu-tock-a-nu-la	Great Chief of the Valley	The Captain	3,300 feet
Wah-wah-le-na		Three Graces	3,400 feet
Pom-pom-pa-sus	Falling Rocks	Three Brothers	3,830 feet
Po-see-nah-Chuck-ca	Large Acorn Cache	Cathedral Spires	2,660 feet
		Sentinel Dome	4,150 feet
Loya		The Sentinel	3,100 feet
		Union Point	2,300 feet
		Moran's Point	2,250 feet
		Glacier Point	3,200 feet

Its general course is northeasterly and southwesterly. The main Merced River runs through it. In many places the walls of the valley are nearly vertical. The mountains surrounding it will average about 4,000 feet in height.

Six days spent in the valley gives one a pretty good chance of seeing it. It is impossible, however, to describe it. It must be seen. "See Naples and die," is a proverb. See Yosemite and live, say we; and after you have seen it, you will still be unable to get your hearers to comprehend the height of its falls, the grandeur of its peaks, and the magnitude of the valley and its surroundings.

It was here, in this great temple of nature, that the Yosemite Assembly was held. A neat chapel was erected by the California

Sunday-school workers, but not fully completed. A bell arrived on Saturday evening, and was soon placed in position, and for the first time

"The sound of the church-going bell"

was heard in the valley.

The Assembly was opened on Saturday evening, June 7th, with an address of welcome by the Rev. Dr. M. M. Gibson, President of the State Association. He said:

We extend a cordial welcome to the Eastern Excursionists. We welcome you to the Pacific State; to the cloudless skies of California; to this temple of nature, the Yosemite Valley, which has been sculptured by the finger of the Almighty; to our hearts which are large enough to hold the sacramental host. California needs the influence which you bring. In the name of the Divine Redeemer we bid you a hearty welcome. We open and pour out the fullness of our hearts before you. In the name of the Executive Committee, in the interests of the Sunday-school, and in the name of Him in whose interests we have assembled, I again bid you a hearty welcome. God grant that from this Assembly streams of influence may go forth that will be felt throughout the State. Two years ago, by unanimous vote, the Committee invited Dr. Vincent to come to California in 1879 and hold two Assemblies. In accordance with that we are assembled this evening, and I now have the pleasure of introducing the Rev. Dr. Vincent, Conductor of the Assembly.

Dr. Vincent conducted the Chautauqua Vesper Service, after which a prayer was offered.

He then spoke of the object of the Assembly, and continued as follows:

We meet in Yosemite. We can hear the thunders of its waterfalls, and look up and see the stars crowning the mountain-tops. This valley has been consecrated by the scientists. I honor them. Those, too, who love the beautiful have come here. We are come to sound the praises of the Most High with the thunders of the waters. We look up and praise Him. Under the inspiration of the moment I could do a very indiscreet thing and talk for an hour—for fifteen minutes—for ten minutes. We are here as scientists, as ministers, as laymen, as neighbors to greet each other, and there are a number of persons from whom I want to hear. I will call on Mr. Rice.

Rev. H. H. Rice, State Secretary, was then introduced.

He spoke of the work of the past two years. God had been leading the way. These Sunday-school meetings had inspired the workers and they wanted to establish the Sunday-school work in California as it was never before established. To save the world by saving the children is the need of California

Rev. Dr. Sinex was next introduced.

After a few words of greeting, he said the mighty rocks, the waterfalls in all their grandeur, were not so grand as God's work on human hearts. He trusted there would be such a feeling exhibited that would make the meetings as good as if they were held in San Francisco or Sacramento. He hoped, as we climed the trails; as we stood upon the mountains; as we were sprinkled with the spray from these mighty waterfalls, we would recognize in all the hand of God.

Rev. Dr. Jackson, of Denver, said he greeted the Assembly as one coming from the centre. He came as one representing the great interior, from Montana to Texas, along the backbone of the continent. He came from the few Sunday-schools of New Mexico, where men and women lash themselves; where they bow to wooden idols; where they crucify themselves on wooden crosses in order to satisfy a guilty conscience; from the Astecs, from the Sun Worshipers, from a country where men worshiped Baal when our fathers were building their woolen churches; from the few Sunday-schools gathered in Utah, and among the Indians. While he came with the greetings of these people, he came also, praying that there might such an influence go from this Assembly as will be a blessing to all.

Galen Clark, State Guardian of the Valley, was then introduced.

He said that in 1851 the first white men entered the valley. A battalion of soldiers came to take the Indians to a reservation. In 1852 some prospectors came. Two were killed and one wounded, after which a party of whites came to chastise the Indians. In 1855 Mr. Hutchings first visited it. The trails were then Indian trails. In 1856 the first trails were opened and tourists came into the valley as campers. In the autumn of 1856 the first house was erected and the following year it was opened as a hotel. In 1864 the United States government gave it to California to be forever held for public use, resort and recreation, and in 1874 the first wagon road was built into the valley.

Rev. Dr. Peltz, after being introduced, said:

One thought has been impressed upon my mind since coming into the valley. "Be still and know the Lord is God." Let it be ours to work with God in his own appointed ways. Let us leave this valley realizing God's greatness as we never did before.

The services were delightfully interspersed with singing, conducted by the Hutchinson Family.

On going into the valley, Mr. Cook, inspired by the magnificent scenery, composed the following, which was known as the Yosemite Doxology, and was sung at nearly every meeting:

> "The hills of God support the skies,
> To God let adoration rise;
> Let hills and skies and heavenly host,
> Praise Father, Son, and Holy Ghost."

Sunday morning the first Sunday-school ever held in the valley, was organized with Rev. H. M. Sanders, of New York, as pastor; Rev. Dr. Peltz, of N. Y., superintendent; Rev. Dr. Gibson, of California, assistant superintendent; Rev. J. M. Allis, of California, chorister; Miss E. P. Fowler, of California, organist; and J. H. Redsecker, secretary. There were one hundred and twenty-six scholars, representing sixteen States, two Territories and the District of Columbia, with twenty visitors. The teachers were, Revs. H. H. Rice, H. W. Brown, A. S. Fiske, Mr. Charles B. Geddes, and Miss Ada Chase, of California; Rev. Dr. Trowbridge, of Mich.; and Mr. Ed. S. Wagoner and Rev. T. J. Ferguson, of Pa.

After Sunday-school, Rev. Dr. Guard preached the dedicatory sermon, and Rev. Joseph Cook made the following dedicatory prayer:

"Almighty God, thou hast consecrated this valley; may we not desecrate it. We are sinners. In the presence of these stupendous revelations of thy power, may we be delivered from contempt of thy word and commandment. Face to face with these precipices may men acquire hearts as upright and downright as these rocks. From thy house, which we dedicate to thee, may thy truth be proclaimed in tones as bold as these hills, and tender as the voice of these waters. What men say here the world will little note, nor long remember; but it will never forget what thou hast said here. May our speech accord with thine. May all discussions of the truth here, echo God. May they reflect Thee as these waters reflect the precipices. We shall pass away and be forgotten, but generation after generation will be represented by those who walk through this valley. We dedicate this house to the religious service of all nations. May artists and poets be inspired here. May statesmen and reformers obtain courage here. May preachers and teachers find strength and tenderness here. When the children of Europe, and of Greece, and of Italy, and of the Holy Land come here, may they meet Thee, and may we meet them in the spirit of Christian brotherhood. When the children of the Yellow Sea come hither, may they find instruction and be treated with justice on the shores of the Pacific. In this holy place wilt thou knit the hearts of all nations to each other and to thyself. The high noon is above our heads, and in the presence of these glorious works of thine, we dedicate this house to Thy service. We give ourselves up to Thee in irreversible, affectionate, total self-surrender. We beseech Thee to fill this temple to the latest generation with the love of God, the grace of our Lord Jesus Christ, and the communion of the Holy Spirit; and this for thine own sake. *Amen.*"

In the afternoon Dr. Vincent preached in front of one of the hotels "On the Way of Salvation," and in the evening Joseph Cook preached in the chapel. Thus the Assembly was formally and profitably opened, and the people prepared for the services of the week.

On Monday morning a "conversation" was held, after which Prof. John Muir, a gentleman who has given many years to a study of the Yosemite Valley and the surrounding mountains, lectured on the "Geological Records of the Valley." Prof. Muir claims that the valley has been formed by glaciers. He says the rocks bear distinct evidence of five glaciers at different periods, some of which were 400 miles long and 70 miles wide. These glaciers carried the rock and debris with them, while the soft earth was deposited in the water and gradually subsided. He presents his arguments so clearly, is so modest and unassuming withal, that you cannot bring yourself to doubt his theory in the absence of other proof to the contrary. He said there were other valleys, not far distant, formed in the same manner, and that a glacier now exists on the Lyall group. On Tuesday Joseph Cook lectured on "Certainties in Religion," and in the evening Prof. Muir lectured on "Mountain Sculpture," which he illustrated by diagrams, and which was as interesting as his lecture on the valley.

Thus the week was made up, with sometimes a day, and again a half-day, spent in excursions, and the rest of the time in lectures, conversations, and the like. One Wednesday evening we had a camp fire, around which the guests in the valley gathered. The fire lighted up the forest beautifully, the great trees cast weird shadows, and the Yosemite Falls thundered just beyond. Rev. Walter W. Hammond opened with a description of Moab, others followed with incidents and descriptions of travel, when Dr. Vincent led a conversation "On the Best Means of Promoting Spirituality in our Churches," Prof. Muir gave an interesting description of the various groves of Big Trees, and at a late hour the meeting closed. Altogether the Yosemite Assembly was one of the most pleasant and instructive of gatherings, combining sight-seeing, with prayer, praise, work, and information. It will long be remembered by the hundreds who were there.

The hotels were crowded. Many with difficulty found sleeping accommodations, but all got enough to eat, and there were but few grumblers, for they expected some inconvenience.

We had been told, "Don't wear a good suit in the valley. A suit once worn in the valley is not fit for further wear." Let me say, you can go into the valley and wear the best clothing you have. Of course you won't do that, nor do you want to take a Saratoga trunk, but you can do so if you wish. We saw no place in the valley where you will get your clothing soiled if you take ordinary care. You will find plenty of dust going in. Do not let any one influence you to put on the worst clothing you have unless you have something better with you. Of course, dress is not everything, but you may feel badly if you have not something better with you. Take water-proof with you, and you can go under the falls if you wish. Read all you can find on the Yosemite before going, and be prepared for a surprise.

NUMBER SIX.

LEAVING THE VALLEY—THE BIG TREES—LOST IN THE MOUNTAINS—MARIPOSA—MERCED—ARRIVAL IN SAN FRANCISCO.

MONTEREY, JULY 2, 1879.

The stage companies had arranged to get all the tourists into the Yosemite Valley in two or three days at the most, and they had the stages ready, and did it, too. But when it came to getting out, we found they were unequal to the task, and could only take one or two stage loads at most, on each route daily, and so we were obliged to get out in small companies.

On Thursday, June 12th, we were up early for our stage was to leave at six o'clock. We waited patiently, or impatiently rather, and at half-past nine, three hours and a-half behind time, the stage pulled up at the door; the passengers were quickly in their places and we were off, out through the valley and slowly toiling up the mountain side. At last Inspiration Point was reached and we had our last look at this famous place which shall remain forever indelibly stamped on the memory. We exclaimed, in the language of one of the native poets:

> "While nature's pulse shall beat the dirge of time,
> Thy domes shall stand—thy glorious waters chime,
> Farewell, Yosemite; thy falls and sunlit towers
> Will rise like visions on my future hours."

We were to be at Clark's at noon. We did not reach there until 5 o'clock and, though it was late, determined to go and see the Big Trees. Mr. Washburn protested slightly, but getting the coach ready, seven of our party got in it, while two of us went on horseback. The distance to the trees is about five miles. We saw them, had quite an adventure, and saw very much more than was in the original programme.

We got as far as the Grizzly Giant, an old veteran of the forest, fully 250 feet high and 100 feet in circumference, passing very many others on our way, and by means of a ladder climbed upon the Fallen Monarch, a tree of immense size fast going to decay.

It was growing late and we urged a return, but the driver wanted to take us through the big tree, which is so large they drive a four-horse stage through it. We went, we saw, and were satisfied that going to see the Big Trees in the evening is not the best time. Your correspondent, who was on horse-back, started for Clark's, hoping the stage would follow. Night came on, and night in the Sierra Nevada mountains, with the Sequoias and tall yellow and sugar pines, means darkness intensified. Urging the horse forward into the darkness, the miles were passed over slowly. Would I ever get out? Were there any grizzlies about? These were questions that, like Banquo's ghost, would not down at one's bidding. Presently hallooing was heard and quickly responded to, supposing it came from the party in the stage. Soon two horsemen, with lanterns, galloped around a curve in the road, inquired for the stage, gave directions about the road, and vanished in the darkness. Plodding forward, at last I saw the glimmering of the lights in the hotel, not more than half a mile distant, and striking a match, found it was half-past nine o'clock. I wound my way around the curves on this wonderfully crooked road, and one hour later drew rein in front of Clark's. But the stage did not come. What of them? Mr. Washburn grew anxious, sent out more men with lanterns, and at ten minutes after one o'clock we were rejoiced to see them return in safety. The driver, in the darkness, drove around a circle in the road, and through the tree some half-dozen times. At last getting out of this, he found his way down the mountain some distance, when the horses got off the road, the stage was nearly upset, and they were obliged to get out, unhitch the horses, and get them back into the road. Further progress in the darkness was impossible, and concluding they would have to remain in the mountain all night, they had built a camp fire and were preparing to make the best of their unpleasant situation. Thus they were found, like the babes in the woods, by the rescuing party, and safely guided to the hotel. There were four ladies in the party, and they acted bravely under such trying circumstances. It was an adventure at the Big trees which will not be forgotten.

While gathered around the camp fire in the Yosemite Valley, Prof. Muir, by request, gave us a description of the Big Trees. The groves are all found between latitude 36 and 38, and never below 5,000, nor above 7,000 feet. There are eight groves of these trees in the Sierra Nevada mountains. The Calaveras, Stanislaus, Merced, Mariposa, Fresno, King's River, North Fork of the Tule River, and the South Fork of the Tule River. They were the first trees to grow after the snow and ice had disappeared, and naturally appropriated to themselves the best soil and most favorable situations. Their age has been variously estimated. Wherever they are found, streams of water are abundant, and some scientists have attributed their immense growth to the abundance of water. Prof. Muir says the size of the trees is not caused by the water, but the water is the result of the trees. The spongy character of the bark —we have seen it over two feet in thickness—and the innumerable roots, are admirably adapted to holding the water, and what has been taken for the cause, is only the effect of their size. Prof. Muir has been in intimate communion with nature for years. He has laid his head close to her beating heart, and his conclusions are the result of careful and thorough investigation.

The Mariposa grove is the largest, containing about 300 trees, and is the property of the State. The Calaveras grove is kept in better condition, we are told, than any other, and has an excellent hotel in the grove. The trees, too, are of greater altitude, being more than 300 feet high, but are smaller in circumference. In the Mariposa grove the Grizzly Giant is the greatest in circumference. There are hundreds, however, which are much higher. The Big Trees all bear the general name of *Sequoia gigantea*, in honor of the Cherokee chief who made an alphabet for his tribe.

They are a species of redwood, and very much resemble the cedar. The cones are small, while those of the sugar pine are of enormous size, and the seeds not nearly so large as a grain of wheat. A friend gave me a few seeds, told me to plant and watch them for the next thousand years. He is fond of a joke, and forgets that my name is not Methuselah.

The next day we were off for Merced, and had a delightful ride through the mountain. The live oaks, on the foothills, look like old orchards at a distance. The moss hangs in festoons from the trees, while the mistletoe is found in great bunches growing upon them.

We passed through the town of Mariposa, where Gen. Fremont's claim is located, which has been in litigation for the past quarter of a century. The town has an abandoned appearance, the mines are not worked, and the entire place has a look of utter dessolation. There is considerable gulch mining done along the streams on this route, principally by the Chinese, who make about a dollar a day. We gathered a handful of dirt, and found it sparkling with small pieces of yellow gold.

Large flocks of Angora goats are found on many of the ranches. They are kept for their long white fleece, which is valuable.

The plains and woods are full of flowers of the most beautiful description. Among them is the snow plant, a bright scarlet flower, the stem of which is a pulpy mass, crystalline like ice, from one to two inches in diameter, and growing like a fungus. Patches of mountain phlox are spread out, decking the sides of the mountain with a flowry carpet, while the escholtzia, with its bright golden flowers, the calechortus or Mariposa lily, a beautiful flower, the mountain pink, with its bright scarlet, and others in infinite variety, add a charm to the scenery. Prof. Muir, who is a botanist as well as a geologist, tells me that not more than five per cent. of the flora of California is found east of the rocky mountains. Everything seems to grow luxuriantly under these favoring skies, and as you look out on the fields, bare and brown, hardly a spear of green grass visible anywhere, you wonder how it is possible. The grass dries on the stem, and is very nutritious, for cattle will feed and fatten on it remarkably well.

We have found the fuchsia, which with us attains a height of two or three feet, grow here up over the sides of the house and have the largest and most perfect flowers. The geraniums grow from six to ten feet high, and have masses of large flowers. The oleander, which we have to take into the house in winter, and the lugging of which I have painful recollections, here remains in the open air the year round. We have seen the Datura—the cultivated variety—growing as a tree, fully fifteen feet high, and bearing flowers from four to six inches in diameter, while the common Datura Stramonium attains a much larger size than with us.

The second day from the valley we reached Merced, and were glad to see the railroad and bid farewell to stage coaches. The next day we took cars for San Francisco, which was reached at noon, and where we soon found the Lick House, a most comfortable hotel. A bath, which we all needed, a dip into our trunks for clean clothing, and we felt ready to see San Francisco, and spend to-morrow—Sunday—in rest and worship.

NUMBER SEVEN.

SAN FRANCISCO—LICK HOUSE—EARLY HISTORY—CHINESE MISSION—DR. KALLOCH'S CHURCH.

SAN FRANCISCO, JULY 8, 1879.

On your arrival in San Francisco you are cordially greeted by the vociferous shouting of the hackmen. who almost lay violent hands on you. You are glad to escape from them, and, securing a carriage, make your way to the hotel you have selected. We had arranged to stop at the Lick House, a quiet, orderly hotel on Montgomery street, in the business portion of the city, and subsequent experience proved that we had made a wise choice. Some of our friends were already there, and Col. John H. Lick, son of the millionaire-philanthropist, an old Lebanonian now stopping in this city, had arranged for our comfort. We were soon made to feel at home, as are all the guests, for there is a home-like air about the Lick House that one experiences at but few hotels.

The house fronts 200 feet on Montgomery street, and extends a distance of 318 feet on Sutter street, and is only three stories high, so that if you are put on the topmost story, as we were not, you are not so very high up in the world. The manager, Mr. Schoenwald, and the clerks, even down to the humblest servant, are exceedingly obliging, and vie with each other in ministering to the comfort of the guests. The hotel is complete in all its apartments, and first-class in every particular.

The dining-room is a marvel of elegance, and is said to be the finest in the world. It is lighted by two large glass chandeliers, each having thirty-six burners. In addition to these, there are twelve three-light burners around the sides which light it up brilliantly. Four large mirrors, eight by ten feet in size, are arranged in the corners, while in the panels on the sides and ends are elegant oil paintings, the size of the mirrors, executed by some of the best artists in the State. They represent "California in 1849," a vessel coming through the Golden Gate; "The Yosemite Falls;" "South Dome," with El Capitan in the foreground; "Sentinel Dome;"

"Mount Shasta;" "The Redwood Forest" in the Russian River Valley; a Scene on the Isthmus of Panama, and others. Having seen the Yosemite, we can say that the canvas representations are true to nature. The dining-room is presided over by Mr. McDermott, who greets the guests with a pleasant smile, places them, and sees that they are properly cared for. The room will comfortably seat 300 guests at one time. We paid our bill, and therefore the notice of this elegant hotel is given gratuitously. There are a number of other hotels in the city, the largest of which is the Palace, where many of our tourists stopped. It is seven stories high, will accommodate 1,200 guests, but is a great barn-like structure. We had occasion to go there a few times on business, and had our head almost taken off by the impudence of the office clerks. You may be sure we gave them as wide a berth as possible after that.

Being thus comfortably fixed, we had time to settle down and study the history of San Francisco, and look at it in its hurry and rush of business.

The first white settlement of San Francisco was made in 1776, by the establishment of a Spanish military post, and a mission of Franciscan Friars to convert the Indians. The Bay of San Francisco was discovered by Father Junipero Serra, a Franciscan Friar, who named it after St. Francis, the patron saint of the order. They erected a cross and took formal possession on the 17th of September, 1770, by religious services and the firing of cannon and musketry from the shore, and the vessel which had arrived a month before.

The mission was maintained until 1835. In 1836 the town of *Yerba Buena*—good herb—was laid out and the first house built by Capt. Richardson, an American. It was simply a large tent supported on four large redwood posts, and covered with a ship's foresail. In 1846 there was not more than twenty houses, with a population of 200. In January, 1848, the name of the place was changed to San Francisco, and by April of the same year it contained 100 houses and 500 people.

In the winter of 1847-8, James W. Marshall, who was digging a mill-race for Capt. Sutter on the American River, a tributary of the

Sacramento, discovered gold. He was wild with excitement when he came to Sutter and made it known. Captain Sutter thought the man crazy, but when he showed him the shining metal all doubts were removed. They agreed to work it together, and leave no one into the secret, but it soon became known, and produced the greatest excitement. By the end of April, 1848, the rush for the gold diggings began, and San Francisco lost most of its male population. In 1849 San Francisco had become a world-famed seaport, and its harbor was filled with the ships of various nations. Each day brought new emigrants either by sea or overland, and at the end of the year 1849, the city had a population of 20,000. By the census of 1850 it had 34,000. In 1854 the gold yield began to decrease, and the city received a business shock, but in 1869 the Comstock and other lodes were discovered and prosperity again restored. San Francisco has had an eventful career. In 1851, 1856, and again in 1877 vigilant committees were formed and took control of the city to rescue and purge it of scoundrels. Their proceedings have always been governed by prudence and justice.

The harbor is one of the finest, it is said, in the world. It is certainly magnificent, and capable of anchoring the navies of the world. It is entered through the Golden Gate, which is about a mile and a quarter wide. The government has a number of forts in and around the harbor. The entrance to the harbor was named the Golden Gate by Gen. Fremont in the spring of 1848, before the gold discoveries. "It was so named because of the rich and fertile country which surrounds its shores, and of the wealth which the commerce of the Pacific would give to the future great city. The name was probably suggested by the Golden Horn of Constantinople, and the discovery of gold afterward has made it significant."

The city has grown rapidly since 1850, and has a number of very handsome business blocks and private residences. Among the notable public buildings are the Mint, Custom House, City Hall, (not yet completed and which will cost over $4,000,000), the Merchants' Exchange, the Mercantile Library, the California and Nevada Banks, and Stock Exchange.

The railroad magnates and bonanza kings have fine private residences on Nob Hill and other portions of the city, as well as elegant summer residences at Menlo Park, about an hour's ride by rail from the city. Many of the houses—fully four-fifths—are built of wood, as they are supposed to be more secure against the shocks of earthquakes, which are by no means of unfrequent occurrence.

We arrived in San Francisco on Saturday afternoon, the 14th of June. In company with friends we went out to see the city, and were attracted by a large crowd. We learned that a drinking-fountain had just been dedicated by Francis Murphy, who has been doing a good work in this city. The fountain was erected by H. D. Coggswell and presented to the city. It is a square shaft of polished granite surmounted by a bronze statue of Benjamin Franklin. It bears the inscription: "Presented by H. D. Coggswell to our boys and girls who will soon take our places and pass on." On three sides were the words "Congress," "Seltzer," "Vichy," and below each was a spigot and a cup. On another side was "Mementoes for the Historical Society in 1979." A number of mementoes were deposited in the base, to be opened a hundred years hence. On the base was the word "Welcome," and the crowd who had gathered about it to partake of the water, gave evidence that they appreciated the welcome. When we remember that there are 8,022 liquor-selling establishments in the city, we may well wish that more of San Francisco's wealthy men would do likewise, and lend their influence to the cause of cold water.

San Francisco is the most cosmopolitan city on the American continent, if not in the world. Almost every nationality is represented here. The American, the English, the French, the German, the Dutch, the Italian, the Portugese, Japanese, Chinese, and how many other nationalities I know not, have been attracted hither by the greed for gold.

Sunday is a grand holiday. We have never seen so much desecration of the Sabbath in any other American city. Stores are open, business is pushed as vigorously, and crime as rampant as on any other day of the week. Boats go out loaded with passengers, with banners flying and bands playing. The cars, too, carry out their thousands; the theaters and concert halls are open; billiard and gambling saloons are in full operation; and the city seems given over to business and pleasure. The churches, of course, are open, and have their share of devout Christian worshipers, but by far the greater portion are off pleasuring, and pay no heed to the command, "Remember the Sabbath day to keep it holy." In our wanderings on Saturday we had seen the Chinese mission building, where Rev. Dr. Loomis' work is conducted. So on Sunday morning we attended the service, which commenced by singing "Praise God," in Chinese. The singing throughout was accompanied by organ music, the playing being done by one of the Chinamen. The 71st Psalm was then read, the Lord's prayer repeated, after which "Jerusalem, my happy home," was sung. Dr. Loomis then led in prayer, and the 69th Psalm was read, the missionary and congregation reading the verses alternately. This was followed by "Rock of Ages," after which one of the converts read the third chapter of Acts. Dr. Loomis then preached a sermon, and was followed in a short exhortation by one of the Chinese brethren, whom we afterward learned was a preacher. Thus far the service was conducted entirely in the Chinese language, and, though we did not understand a word, it was very interesting. They then sang "I love to tell the story" in English, and did remarkably well. The Lord's prayer was repeated and the doxology sung, both in English, and the services closed. The women come in by a side door and sit apart from the men behind curtains, so that they cannot be seen. Dr. Loomis has been a missionary since 1844, and for the past twenty years has been engaged in missionary work among the Chinese in this city. Immediately after the preaching service they had a Sunday-school session, but another engagement prevented our staying. This mission is under the care of the Presbyterian Church. They have about a 120 converts, a Young Men's Christian Association, Sabbath and day schools, and are doing a good work. We were cordially greeted by our Chinese brethren, some of whom spoke English very well.

We afterwards learned that there are three Chinese missions in this city, the others being conducted by the Methodist and Congregational Churches. In the afternoon we accompanied Dr. Vincent to several of the Methodist Sunday-schools, and had the pleasure of hearing him make several addresses. He is a pleasant speaker, knows how to talk to young people, as well as old, and holds their attention throughout. In the evening we went to hear Dr. Kalloch, a Baptist minister, who has since been nominated by the Kearney party for mayor of the city. His church is built like a theatre, and will hold 2,500 people. He is a great sensational character, and they are drawn thither because of this. We never were in a church where there appeared to be less worship. He began the service by reading extracts from letters and the press, and commenting on them to the infinite amusement of his audience, which applauded when anything pleased them. After this a lady sang a solo, which was so good that the audience *encored* and she had to repeat it. The preacher then announced his text, and throughout the sermon there were frequent demonstrations of applause. The sermon ended, a short prayer was said, after which the audience began to disperse without waiting for the closing hymn or the benediction, which, however, were gone through with. To call it worship is a misnomer. One of our lady tourists who was there told me she was shocked at the demonstrations of the audience, and turning to a lady who was sitting beside her, asked, "Do they conduct their services always in this way?" "Indeed I do not know. I am a stranger here, and I have promised the Lord that if he lets me get out of this, I'll never go into such a place again," was the reply she received.

But my letter is already of sufficient length. The sights of the city, our sail on the bay, the Chinese quarter, and the Chinese theatre, with other matters of interest, will have to wait for our next.

NUMBER EIGHT.

THE CHINESE QUESTION—CHINATOWN—THE THEATRE— STREET RAILWAYS—YACHTING—DIAMOND PALACE— MARKETS.

SAN FRANCISCO, JULY 9, 1879.

The Chinese question is a problem in the social and political future of California that will require a wise and liberal statesmanship to adjust. "The Chinese must go " is the chorus shouted by Kearney and his followers, while the Chinese as positively say they will not go. They are here by treaty stipulation with the United States government, and know and will maintain their rights. They say that for years they were alone, having no intercourse with the outside world, and desired to have none. They claim it was forced on them at the cannon's mouth by the European and American nations, and they had to accept. They purpose keeping their part of the treaty faithfully, and expect other nations to do the same. In this they are right. It does seem a piece of presumption for men like Kearney and his ignorant followers, composed as they largely are of the worst elements of society, and they themselves foreigners who are here by sufferance of the liberal policy of the government, to assume to dictate to the American nation its foreign policy, and say who shall or who shall not come or stay.

It is true the Chinese are heathen, do not engage in Sand-Lot demonstrations on the Sabbath-day and disturb the public peace. It is true they do not drink whiskey at corner-groggeries, swill German beer in some public garden, talk of a division of property and raise the red flag of communism; do not incite to incendiarism, riot or plunder; but still they must go—and why? Because by their patience, their plodding and their willingness to do an honest day's work for fair wages they are displacing, to some extent, the striking, brawling white laborer, who is unwilling to work for less than $2.50 to $4 per day. It is a great pity this is so, but it is nevertheless a fact. Whether it would be wise to place some restriction on their further coming is a question, but why not accord them the same privileges extended to others? Will a few hundred thousand Chinamen drive forty millions of people to the wall? I think not.

In conversation with a gentleman of wealth and position, he told me that a legislative committee appointed to investigate the subject reported that they were *too economical, too industrious, too apt*, and that they worked *too cheap*. These were the only causes of complaint which could be lodged against them.

"How do you like John?" we asked a lady who employs several as domestic servants. "Indeed I do not know how I would get along without them. I have tried help of all kinds, and in the midst of harvest, when we had our hardest work, they have left me, and I was obliged to do the work myself. We tried Irish women, and in less than two weeks we had to carry several of them out, for they got drunk. They drank wine vinegar, so strong that no one else would have thought of touching it. You see we turn all our grapes into vinegar—wine vinegar. At last I was forced to get Chinamen, and since then we have had no trouble. They are honest, faithful, and learn quickly." This is the testimony of many others with whom I have spoken.

Of course no Eastern tourist visits San Francisco without going to see Chinatown. It is in the centre of the city, and is a most wonderful part of it. We saw its various phases, and in daytime visited its stores, talked with the people, and saw nothing so very shocking. But you want to see it at night. Accompanied by a policeman some half-dozen of us were piloted through the alleys, up rickety stairs, down into dark, deep cellars, and into small rooms in which twenty to thirty men pack themselves like sardines and sleep without ventilation. We went into the opium dens where men were smoking the drug, and some were lying curled up in blankets asleep under its influence. The sights were disgusting and shocking, and you wonder how it is possible for any human beings to live thus. But it is not worse than one could see among other nationalities in any of our large cities. It is not any worse, certainly, than to see the pigs and goats in one end of the shanty while parents and children occupy the other. You might as well take a stranger through Bedford and Baker streets in Philadelphia, or through the slums of any of our cities, and tell him Americans live thus. It would be a libel on American civilization. It is surely not as shocking as the French quarter, where vice lifts its hydra head in open day. We also visited Chinatown under the guidance of our friend Ching Yuen, a gentleman and a Christian, and were shown a very different aspect of affairs. The wholesale and retail merchants were very pleasant, and the stores light and airy. We also had the pleasure of calling on the Chinese Consul, and found him and his assistants very pleasant, his chief clerk speaking English quite fluently. Ching Yuen took us to his home, which was nicely furnished, while on the walls we observed such mottoes as "God bless our home," and "The Lord is risen." His wife is a fine-looking lady, was dressed in Chinese costume, and speaks English quite well. We also visited the Chinese theatre, which should not be missed by those who visit San Francisco. You may not understand the plays, for they are representations of Chinese history, and continue through months. There is no drop-curtain, and no scenery whatever. The orchestra sits on the stage, while the music is the most inharmonious and discordant you ever heard. The stage property is very meagre, consisting of a cheap, square table and a few plain chairs, but they are made to answer many purposes. A chair turned on its side represented a well, while a chair stood on the table and covered with a cloth represented a throne for the king. The acrobatic performance is truly wonderful, while their fencing is grand, for, be it remembered, the Chinaman fights with two swords. The audience sit and smoke, watch the play with great interest, never applaud, and hardly ever smile.

Justice Field, of the U. S. Court, has just rendered an important decision. The sheriff of San Francisco cut off the queue of a Chinaman who had been imprisoned for five days. The Chinaman brought suit, laying his damages at $10,000, and the courts have decided favorably for him. The decision has created great comment and much bitter feeling.

San Francisco has a perfect network of street railways, and you can reach any part of the city for five cents. There are several streets which have cable roads, on which the cars are noiselessly moved by some invisible power. We were shown the machinery which moves the cars on the California street road. They use 25,000 feet of cable, which runs in the centre of the track, revolved horizontally around immense iron wheels at the ends of the road and in the engine-room. A dummy, to which the cars are attached, is fitted with grip, brakes and levers. The engineer draws a lever which fastens the grip to the revolving cable and the car is propelled forward. When he wants to stop the grip is loosed and the brakes applied. The two engines, each 250 horse-power, are located under the road on Larkin street, about midway between the termini. The machinery is of the most complete character, and so arranged that it automatically takes up any slack in the cable. The grade on this road is in many places one foot elevation in every five feet, so that it would be impossible to use horses.

We drove to the Cliff House, through the park, which, in years to come, will be a handsome place. A large conservatory, which James Lick purchased with the intention of erecting on his lands near San Jose, was bought from the trustees by several of the city's public-spirited citizens and presented to the park. It contains a variety of choice flowers, some of which, especially the aquatic plants, are very rare. From the Cliff House you get a fine view of the Pacific ocean and the seal rocks, on which are hundreds of the sea monsters quietly lounging about sunning themselves, or sporting in the water. They are carefully guarded by the authorities.

The harbor of San Francisco is one of the finest on the continent. Through the kindness of Mr. J. Clem Uhler, an old Lebanonian, we spent a day most delightfully in the yacht Emerald, visiting the boat-house of the San Francisco Yacht Club, where we lunched, and thence to Fort Alcatraz, where we saw a dress parade, where the officers gathered handsome bouquets for the ladies, and entertained us all as handsomely as gallant officers know how.

Montgomery street is the Broadway or Chestnut street of San

Francisco, and here are the elegant stores of the city. The most magnificent jewelry store we ever saw is the Diamond Palace of Col. Andrews. It sparkles with rare gems of value, while the jewelry is of the most artistic character, displaying the skill and genius of the proprietor. It is of the frescoing that I wish particularly to speak. They are works of art worthy of the brain that conceived, and the hand that painted them. They represent "Rebekah at the well," "Queen Esther," arrayed in royal robes, while her crown, her bracelets, her girdle and her ear-rings sparkle with brilliant diamonds; "Deborah, the Prophetess," "Jeptha's daughter," "Delilah," "The Egyptian girl," and "The Woman of Samaria," complete the frescoes. In the girdle or head-dress of each are appropriate gems. The sides are plate-glass mirrors, while the woodwork is finished in black and gold.

We had the pleasure of meeting John S. Hittell, Esq., editor of the *Alta,* and author of several works on California. His *Resources of California,* a copy of which I have with the author's compliments, is a work of value, and has been largely quoted by writers. He is one of the early pioneers, and a prominent member and historian of the Pioneer Society.

Col. John H. Lick, son of the millionaire whose name is familiar in connection with his large bequests, also showed us many acts of kindness. He is a resident of Lebanon, and is only staying temporarily in San Francisco.

You have heard of California fruit. Perhaps you have eaten of it, but you have never seen it in the San Francisco markets. San Francisco has strawberries the year round; large luscious berries that make one's "mouth water" to look at. And such cherries! Well, you can make two bites of one of them with ease. Other fruits in great abundance are to be found in the markets, and you inwardly say, "If it were not three thousand miles, I would like to send some home that friends might see and taste."

The Stock Exchange is a perfect bedlam to a stranger. It is quite amusing to see the brokers buying and selling. They jump at each other as if they were going to have a real rough-and-tumble fight. A gentleman who went in with his little daughter, found it impossible to prevent her screaming, for she thought they were going to have a regular fisticuff. And I am not surprised, for they act sometimes like uncaged wild beasts.

The Hoodlum is an institution peculiar to San Francisco, and vary in age from five to twenty years. They are a bad element; sleep in, around and under the wharves like rats; will shoot a policeman as quickly as they would a dog; pull John Chinaman's queue as if it were a door-bell, and behave generally like untamed savages. They are a most vicious lot, and are going from bad to worse. They live by stealing, begging and pocket-picking.

NUMBER NINE.

SAN RAFAEL—ON THE ROAD TO THE GEYSERS—THE GEYSERS—FOSS—NAPA VALLEY—GRAPE CULTURE AND WINE MAKING.

SAN FRANCISCO, JULY 10, 1879.

Among the marvelous natural wonders with which California abounds there is, perhaps not one—Yosemite excepted—that presents more attractions for the tourist than the great Geysers, as they are called, though they are really not Geysers, strictly speaking, but a series of hot springs and steam jets issuing out of the side of a mountain. They are well worth a visit, as the route takes you through some of the finest valleys of this land of wonders.

Our arrangements for the trip were all made by our friend, Col. John H. Lick, and took us through the famous Sonoma and Russian Valleys, and back to San Francisco by the Napa Valley, famous as the great grape-growing region of the State. In fact we "swung around the circle."

The Rev. Mr. Ferguson, of Cumberland county, and your correspondent started in advance of the rest of the party and spent the night in San Rafael, a beautiful little town, fifteen miles north of San Francisco and eight miles from the ocean. It is noted as one of the sanitariums of the State and is much sought as a health resort, having less fog and wind than any other town close to San Francisco. It is near the foot of Tamalpais mountain. Some residents of San Francisco whom we met here, and to whom we suggested that it was hardly necessary to leave the city with its delightfully cool breezes, told us they came away to get warm. There is an air of comfort, home-life and leisure about San Rafael, with its cottages, and yards full of beautiful flowers, that does not exist in the great city across the bay.

The next morning we joined our friends and were soon whirling along through the beautiful Sonoma Valley, passing the outskirts of Petaluma, and farther on stopping for a few minutes in the beautiful town of Santa Rosa, which offers many inducements for tourists to stop, but as our time was limited, we were obliged to go on. Santa Rosa, we are informed, contains a famous "rose-tree which at one time contained 20,000 blossoms, and though shorn of much of its beauty, still remains a gigantic bush."

We pass from the Sonoma into the Russian River Valley, with the river gliding smoothly on its way to the ocean, very much diminished in size because of the dry weather, but in winter it is a stream of considerable size. We at length reach Cloverdale, the terminus of the railroad, and take stages for the Geysers, fourteen miles distant.

We cross the Russian river, and enter the mouth of the canyon from which issues the Pluton river on its way from the Geysers. The scenery is of the wildest description, and the road one of the most dangerous we have yet seen. A short distance from the mouth of the canyon we are shown profile rock, a huge projection of rock on the side of the mountain which bears a strong resemblance to a human face.

We have entered the canyon, and our road is cut along its side, while hundreds of feet below is the river. The timid or nervous traveler should take a seat next the mountain, for he cannot look

ACROSS THE CONTINENT. 61

down the abrupt declivity along which we travel, without a shudder at the possibility of an accident. Should the driver be careless, or the horses become unmanageable, we would be plunged into the yawning abyss below a distance of several hundred feet.

As we pass further on the canyon opens out, and fine grazing land, tall pines, and the beautiful mandrona and manzanita, with their red bark and green foliage, abound in great variety. We also pass several deserted quicksilver mines, which are not now worked as the price of the metal will not pay for the labor. At last, after a dangerous, warm and dusty ride, we see jets of steam issuing out of the mountain side, and a few minutes later our stage stops in front of the Geyser Hotel. We wash off the dust of travel, and are ready to take a short walk through a portion of the canyon to the bath-house, where they have steam baths, the steam being supplied from the hillside. Having seen the bath-house, the next thing is to take a steam bath. You disrobe, enter a close, box-like room, turn on the steam, and in a few moments you find the perspiration streaming from every pore. After you have lost some twenty pounds, more or less, you enter another room, take a shower bath, then a plunge bath, and come forth a cleaner—and if "cleanliness is next to godliness"—a better person than when you went in.

By this time the stages on the Calistoga road arrive, and we find they have brought about forty of our tourists, and the hotel is overcrowded. Mr. Forsythe, however, did handsomely by our little party, and we were nicely accommodated.

The next morning we start to see the wonders of the Geysers. We find the canyon full of springs, boiling with heat, and emitting large quantities of steam, with a roaring, hissing noise. There is an eye-water spring, which is said to possess wonderful curative properties for all diseases of the eye, as well as for all cutaneous diseases. We also see the devil's arm-chair, which is a hollowed-out rock, and forms a comfortable seat. We wonder why everything is named after the devil? They have even a mount Diabolo. Passing on up the canyon we are soon brought into the devil's kitchen, where there is a terrible hissing noise produced by the steam issuing from all sides of the mountain, while water, black as ink, and heated to the boiling point, bubbles up on every side. The witches' cauldron is the largest spring in the canyon. It is about ten feet across, very deep, and very black. The water is boiling hot, and is raised to a distance of several feet. It seethes and boils at a furious rate, while just beside it flows a stream of beautifully clear and cold water, so that you may stoop down and dip one hand into boiling, and the other into cold water.

The canyon is nature's grand chemical laboratory, for here you may find in process of manufacture, sulphate of magnesia (epsom salts), sulphate of iron (copperas), sulphate of aluminum (alum), and sulphate of copper (blue vitriol), as these various minerals are found here, and are combined with the sulphur which abounds in the water.

Passing out of the canyon we descend the side of the mountain and pass the "steamboat," an opening about eight inches in diameter in the mountain, from whence issues the steam with a loud hissing noise like that made by a steam engine. Large columns of steam rise to a height of from fifty to two hundred feet. We pass over the Modoc lava beds, so called because of the lava they contain, and not because the Modocs were ever here.

You have seen the Geysers, and are impressed with this great natural wonder. You return to the hotel, are ready for breakfast, and ready also to leave for Fossville. But the stages are crowded with those who came in them, and you don't want to crowd in and crowd some of them out, as did a Universalist minister from San Francisco. But what else can you expect? So you wait for Foss to send up a special, as he did for our party.

Our return is by way of Calistoga, and we find the same narrow road along the side of the hill, while hundreds of feet below us is the deep gorge into which you look and shudder, fearful lest some slight mishap may plunge your stage and yourself into the depths below, from which there is no hope of escape with your life. At last we reach the summit of the mountain, and have a glorious view of the Russian, Sonoma and Napa Valleys. It is impossible to describe it. Stretching away for miles and miles, as far as the eye can reach, is one broad expanse of mountain and plain, while away off in the distance, bounding our utmost view, is the dim outline of the Pacific Ocean. "Grand! magnificent! glorious!" and like exclamations burst from each, and you feel repaid for all the dangers through which you have passed. We descend the mountain into the beautiful Napa Valley, pass a number of vineyards and winehouses, in which the beverage is stored, but as we were all temperance people we did not stop to sample it. By evening we reach Fossville, where resides Clark Foss, the famous stage-driver of the Pacific coast. He is a large muscular man, six feet high and weighs 240 pounds. He has been driving stage for about twenty-five years, and has the reputation of being the best "whip" on the coast. He knows how to keep a hotel, too, and tired and hungry as we were, we enjoyed the excellent supper he set before us, and the clean spring-beds which were enough of themselves to invite sleep. Foss is a character, and entertained us with quaint descriptions of people he had driven, showed us his horses and stages, and promised to drive us to Calistoga in the morning. The breakfast, under the skillful manipulations of Mrs. Foss, like the supper, was so appetizing that you couldn't help enjoy it, after which we were ready for the drive.

The parson and your correspondent were accorded the seats of honor alongside the driver. Gathering up the lines in one hand with a firm grip, he gave the long-lashed whip a peculiar twirl, and we heard an explosion like that of a pistol. The horses started at a brisk trot, and we bade adieu to Fossville and settled ourselves for a lively ride. Foss' horses know their driver and obey his every word. When a favorable stretch of road was reached, he called out "Shake! Shake one!" and away they flew into a rapid run for about half a mile. "Down," came the word from our driver, and in an instant the running gate is changed to a trot. "Way down," again exclaims Foss, and the horses come to a walk. It is truly wonderful how he has his horses under command; and he assured us that you cannot do anything with a horse until you have gained his love. That seems to be the secret of his command over his horses. Suddenly we came to a tree standing in the middle of the road, and before we knew it the stage and four were flying around it in a circle. Again he circled around the tree, turning the stage and four horses in a circle of less than thirty feet diameter. It is six and a half miles from Foss' to Calistoga, and we drove it in thirty-one minutes, having seen some of Foss' driving, which is truly marvelous.

At Calistoga we took the cars for Vallejo, passing through St. Helena, a famous summer resort and sanitary town, and through Napa, the county seat, famous for its college for young ladies. Large fields covered with grape vines line either side of the road. The vines are not permitted to grow to a greater height than four or five feet, are tied to a stake and the entire growth forced into the fruit. On the train we met one of the largest vintners in the State, who makes 225,000 gallons of wine annually. He told us that eighteen years ago there was but one vineyard of ten acres in the Napa Valley. Last year, in Napa county alone, there were 2,000,000 gallons of wine made. It requires thirteen pounds of grapes to make one gallon of wine, and the wine is sold at from 32 to 75 cents per gallon. Very little of it is sold less than a year old, and much is stored from five to ten years, which greatly increases the price. Land in the Napa Valley sells from $60 to $150 per acre, and hillside from $10 to $50 per acre.

Near Napa we got a fine view of the State Insane Asylum, which is a series of large quadrilateral buildings, and where, we were informed, those unfortunate persons are very kindly cared for. There is another similar institution at Stockton. By nine o'clock we reached Vallejo, where we took the boat down the bay, and were landed at the wharf, and were back to our comfortable hotel by noon, greatly delighted with our trip to the Geysers.

In going to the Geysers you can go by either of these routes, but we say, go by one and return by the other, as the fare is only two dollars more.

NUMBER TEN.

ON THE OCEAN—SEA SICKNESS—SANTA BARBARA—COL. HOLLISTER'S RANCH—ALONG THE COAST.

SAN FRANCISCO, JULY 11, 1879.

On Thursday, June 26th, we left San Francisco on board the Pacific Coast Steamship Company's steamer, The Senator, for a trip down the coast. By eight o'clock some two hundred and fifty passengers had gathered on board, a large majority of whom were our tourists. The signal was given, the steamer loosed from her moorings, and swung out into the beautiful San Francisco Bay. We steamed past the shipping in the harbor, passed Fort Alcatraz with its frowning guns, and out through the Golden Gate on to the broad bosom of the trackless Pacific ocean. The passengers were on deck to get a view of the bay and the Golden Gate, but as we crossed the bar the vessel was pitched and tossed on the waves so that many of them were glad to get indoors, while many others began to show signs of weakening. It wasn't very long before the cabins, deck and saloon were full of passengers, who, like the Frenchman. "didn't care whether the porter took his boots, his hat, his coat, his everything, for he knew he would never want them any more." A more distressed-looking crowd I have never seen.

When twelve o'clock arrived, and lunch was announced, there were only about fifty out of the two hundred and fifty, to respond to the announcement. Your correspondent wouldn't and didn't get sick, much to the disappointment of some of his friends. The sick were handsomely serenaded by one of the tourists. Seeing a hand organ on deck, he secured it, and strapping it over his shoulder, made the circuit of the vessel, grinding out the melodious music to the infinite amusement of even the sick. Others held their hats, but the musician was not rewarded, I am sorry to say.

The day was a delightful one, and those who were well enough enjoyed it greatly. On our left was the coast, with its range of mountains, along which we skirted at a respectful distance, while on our right stretched the great Pacific, until sea and sky seemed to meet.

About mid-day, away off to our right, we saw the spouting of a whale, the water rising in two columns to quite a height. The captain informed us that this was not an infrequent thing. The porpoises occasionally came near our vessel and tossed themselves in the air, and at one time quite a school of them was seen.

In the afternoon we reached Santa Cruz, famous as a watering place, where our boat stopped to discharge part of her cargo and take on more freight. We had an opportunity of going ashore, taking a look at the town, or that part of it to be seen along the beach, and permit some of the passengers to gather shells and moss. The vessel then steered across Monterey Bay direct for Monterey, near which the Sunday-school Assembly was held. We reached Monterey by six o'clock in the evening, where some two hundred of our passengers landed, glad that they could again set foot on *terrâ firma*, and some of them inwardly vowing they would never again "sail the ocean blue."

We pushed out from land, and headed the vessel for the south. bound for Santa Barbara, two hundred and eighty-eight miles from San Francisco, and famous as a great sanitary resort, especially for those afflicted with pulmonary diseases. San Louis Obispo, and other ports are passed during the night, and the next afternoon we passed Point Conception light-house, and then turned directly east, as you will see by looking at the map. Those who had been sick were now well over it, and we had a pleasant and merry company, who greatly enjoyed the voyage. About nine o'clock at night we reached Santa Barbara, and were met at the wharf by George S. Bowman, Esq., a young attorney of Lebanon, who is now there for his health. We went at once to the Arlington, which we found to be a large and comfortable hotel. The town is pleasantly located and has a population of about 6,000. Near the town is the Old Mission, established more than a hundred years ago. The walls are of adobe brick, very thick, and the buildings are in good state of preservation. The chapel has a number of old paintings, some of which, they claim, are by old masters, while others are nothing but daubs. The ceiling was frescoed by the Indians and is quite artistic, when we remember who did it. There are a number of buildings occupied by the monks, into several of which we ventured, and found them quite comfortable. They were at vesper service when we arrived, and we found that they had left an interesting game of chess to engage in prayer. We were sorely tempted to change the position of some of the men, but forbore, mindful of the pleasure they were having. We were told that attached to the church was a large corral, into which they used to get the Indians, keep them until they had christianized them by sprinkling with holy water, and then turn them out, or put them to work.

Through the kindness of Mr. Bowman and his friend Mr. Bagg, we were driven to the country, and had the pleasure of seeing Col. Hollister's famous ranche of 60,000 acres. He has large orchards of almond, English walnut, orange, lemon, lime, olive and apricot trees, besides other fruits in great variety. His apricots were just ripe, and the trees were bending under their weight of fruit. They hung in clusters, much like bunches of grapes. We were shown some strawberry plants, and ate some of the berries, that were planted last December. In January, one month later, they were in blossom, and in February they fruited, two months after planting. They were the "Monarch of the West," very large and of fine flavor. We saw also some apple trees in fruit and blossom at the same time. On his ranche there are rare tropical and semi-tropical plants, which do exceedingly well. The Japanese persimmon is quite a curiosity. The trees were not more than four feet high, and the persimmons when ripe weigh from one-half to three-quarters of a pound each.

The climate of Santa Barbara is wonderful, and not only beneficial for invalids, but excellent for vegetation. Roses are in bloom the year round, and our annual plants there become perennial. We saw some melon vines on Col. Hollister's ranche that were planted four years ago, and they were bearing this season. Potatoes, we were told by a reliable gentleman, grow and bear for four years, when the vines die as if from exhaustion. From Col. Hollister's we drove over to Mr. Bagg's ranche, where we rested for several hours, and had an elegant lunch. Here is where our friend, Mr. Bowman, is stopping, and it is a most delightful place. The temperature at noonday was seventy degrees, while the nights are sufficiently cool for blankets. The ranche is located at the head of a canyon, and from the verandah you have a magnificent view of the ocean and a portion of Santa Cruz island. The California quail and other game are very abundant, and as we drove to the ranche a fine, large deer, with head erect, bounded across the road in front of us, and went flying up the mountain out of sight.

The boats do not run daily to and from Santa Barbara. We reached it on Friday, and the Senator returned again on Saturday evening. As we wanted to get to the Monterey Assembly, we were obliged to return by the Senator, thus limiting our visit to this delightful place.

On our return from the country, we found the steamer lying at the wharf. Bidding adieu to friends who had determined to remain until the following Thursday, we stepped aboard, and soon after were steaming away from the town. When night came on, twenty-four miles distant, we saw the light from Point Conception flashing out its danger signal, and directing the mariner how to steer his vessel.

We stop at Cayucos, from which port the people of Lompoc ship their goods. Lompoc is a temperance community two hundred and sixty miles south of San Francisco. The community was started four years ago, and now has a population of about 2,000. The land was bought by a company, and in selling to settlers it is stipulated in the deeds that no liquor is to be sold or manufactured on the premises. They have no policemen and there are no arrests for drunken or disorderly conduct.

The crops raised are barley, beans, potatoes and squashes. Beans yield an average of one and a half to one and three-quarter tons to the acre, and bring about $30 per ton. The average potato yield is 200 bushels to the acre, and bring about twenty-five cents a bushel.

Squashes will yield thirty tons to the acre, and are raised for feeding and fattening hogs. The mangel-wurzel beet will produce fifty tons to the acre, and are used as food for stock. Single beets will grow to an enormous size, weighing as much as one hundred pounds. These figures may seem an exaggeration, but they were given me as reliable by a gentleman whom I met on the boat, and were subsequently corroborated by another with whom I conversed, and whom I know to be a person of veracity.

We had a delightful sail to Monterey, which we reached on Monday morning.

The Senator is a staunch vessel, commanded by Captain W. E. Plummer, a genial, gentlemanly person, who tries to make all his passengers comfortable, looks after their wants and gives them all possible information. He never swears and does not permit any of the men under him to use profane language. We parted from him reluctantly, and can assure our readers that if they ever fall into the captain's hands they will be most kindly cared for. The mate, the purser, the steward, and all, seem to partake of the nature of the commander, and were exceedingly pleasant.

Long may "the gallant captain of the Senator" continue to "sail the ocean blue."

NUMBER ELEVEN.

MONTEREY—THE OLD MISSION—THE ASSEMBLY—SAN JOSE—ALMADEN QUICKSILVER MINE.

DAVISVILLE, CAL., JULY 14, 1879.

On Monday morning, June 30th, our steamer drew alongside the wharf at Monterey, and we stepped ashore. Monterey is, perhaps, the oldest town in the State, and has an advantage over any other town that we saw. When it was built,—well, they finished it, for there have been no improvements since. The streets run in every imaginable irregular way, as though some monster hand had held them up over the town and dropped them down, as children do jack-straws. Along these streets the old adobe houses were built, and many of them were inclosed by high walls covered with tiles. The town has several hundred houses, but none of modern construction. It has one Protestant church (Episcopal), which will hold two hundred people. The Catholic church is a fine adobe building, built in 1794, similar in construction to all the old Catholic churches of that period, being quite long and narrow, with Indian frescoing. The bay is large, and there is quite a fine stretch of beach. The town dates back to 1602, when Viscaino, a Mexican navigator, first landed in the harbor, and held worship. His expedition was sent out by the Count de Monterey, Viceroy of Mexico, and he named the place in honor of the Viceroy. On the 3d of July, 1770, the Franciscan fathers landed at Monterey and established their mission in a beautiful valley, about four miles from the site of the present town. The spot where they landed and held worship is marked by a large wooden cross, bearing the date.

Monterey was the first capital of the State of California, and the first town over which the American flag was hoisted when Commodore Sloat took possession of the country in the name of the United States. He was at Mazatlan, and on the 31st of May, 1846, heard of General Taylor's victories at Palo Alto and Resaca de la Palma, on the 8th and 9th of the same month. He waited a week for the confirmation of the news, and then set sail for Monterey, reaching there July 1st. The people were becoming impatient of Mexican rule, and the country was ready for a change of government. England looked longingly toward California, and waited only a fitting opportunity to seize the prize. Gen. Fremont was in the country with a small exploring expedition. He had several disputes with the local authorities, and on the 14th of June, 1846, some of his command, aided by volunteers, captured the town of Sonoma. Leaving a small garrison, Gen. Fremont moved into the San Joaquin Valley, and was on his way toward Oregon when Com. Sloat arrived in Monterey harbor. He spent a week in consultation with the authorities of the town, and on the 7th of July, 1846, he landed his forces, hoisted the American flag, and took possession of the country. Eight days afterward the English ship of war, Collingwood, commanded by Admiral Seymour, came into the harbor, when the admiral discovered that the prize for which they had been looking and planning, had fallen into the hands of the Americans. The old building over which the flag was hoisted is still standing, and on the Fourth of July, when we left Monterey, the stars and stripes were floating from the flagstaff.

The building in which the first Legislature met is an old adobe, two stories, and is in a rickety condition. The State-house, built later, is now used as the public school building. The Old Mission, built by the Franciscan fathers in 1770-71, is in a beautiful valley across the mountain, and commands a magnificent view of the ocean. The buildings inclosed a number of acres, but nothing but ruins remain. A portion of the walls are still standing; the tower and belfry remain, but their glory have long since departed. The bell is now used by the church in Monterey, while the old pictures which formerly hung in the Mission, adorn its walls. On the walls we saw this inscription, by an unknown hand:

> "Change and decay on every hand I see:
> O thou who changest not, abide, abide with me."

Two miles from Monterey, along the Pacific ocean, is a beautiful grove, which has been nicely fitted up as a camp ground by the Methodists. There are some nice cottages, a number of canvas and board tents, a store, postoffice, and a large, comfortable parlor, with Brussels carpet, open fire-place, with a cheerful log fire, and comfortable chairs. On the walls, in letters of evergreen, were the words, "The Pacific greets the Atlantic," and "Welcome." About a mile distant, on a point of land, is the Monterey light-house, a substantial stone building with its revolving light as a beacon to the seafaring. Several miles distant are Moss Beach, Point Lopos, Cypress Point, and other places of interest, along which many wandered, gathering moss, abalone, sea-urchin, and other marine shells. It was a grand sight to sit on the rocks and watch the ebb and flow of the ocean. The waves would hurl themselves against the rocks with a crashing noise, only to be broken into foam. The words of Tennyson's poem involuntarily came to mind:

> " Break, break, break,
> On thy cold, grey stones, O sea!
> And I would that my heart could utter
> The thoughts that arise in me."

Here, with the ocean mingling its ceaseless roar with the songs and praises of the people, is where the Sunday School Assembly was held, conducted by the Revs. Drs. Vincent and Peltz.

The Assembly began Friday evening, June 27th, but I did not reach the ground until the Monday following. On Monday we had normal instruction in Bible History and Geography, by the Rev. Dr. Vincent, and Bible Construction by the Rev. Dr. Peltz, a temperance meeting, conducted by the Rev. Dr. Briggs, of San Francisco, and a conversation on a Good Sunday-school Programme, lead by the Rev. Dr. Willey of Santa Cruz. In the evening Dr. Vincent lectured on "New Departures." The lecture was full of advanced ideas. He suggested graduating the children out of the Sunday-school at fifteen years of age, and putting them with the men and women into a department to be called the Assembly. Let this be a place of culture and advancement; provide for a course of study and reading, and have week-day services as well as Sunday services. Provide books and papers full of helpfulness and healthfulness, and the boys and girls will not drift away from the school nor have time for crowding their minds with the pernicious literature thrown out by the secular press. The lecture was full of excellent thoughts and suggestions, but my limited space will not admit of even a condensed report.

Tuesday we had a lecture on the "Uses of the Bible and Bible Helps," by the Rev. H. H. Rice, of Sacramento, secretary of the Association. He spoke of the progress of Bible science, as being equal with material science—we must progress if we would be worthy of our vocation as teachers—of the advancement made in the study of the Greek and Hebrew texts, and the great labor expended in getting the very best translations. He urged the study of the Scriptures, first as a Christian, and then as a teacher, suggesting that the teacher have a general comprehensive knowledge of the Book. Other gentlemen spoke on the same subject, which was one of interest. Other lectures and addresses filled in the day. In the evening Dr. Vincent held a delightful service by the sea, and at night delivered his lecture on "That Boy." No one can report it, for the earnestness, the tender tone of voice, the capital hits, and the excellent advice, cannot be put on paper. It must be heard.

Wednesday and Thursday were days of good solid Sunday-school work, conducted by Dr. Peltz, Dr. Vincent being obliged to leave for home. Addresses on various topics were delivered by Dr. Wythe, Prof. Norton, Dr. Gibson, president of the Association, Dr. Bentley, Rev. A. S. Fiske, Dr. Peltz and others. Dr. Peltz spoke on Primary Classes. He said he much preferred the name Primary Classes to that of Infant Classes. He urged that teachers should have respect to the physical necessities of the primary scholars. They should have bright, light, cheerful rooms with good seats, and plenty of air. The scholars are full of vital energy, and cannot be quiet very long. Their muscles should be brought into play in an orderly manner. This can be done by having them rise up to sing, having marching songs, in which they march in an orderly way up and down the aisles. If they are given good physical exercise you will not have to beg of them to keep quiet. He suggested that the best teachers should be employed as primary class teachers. He also urged care in the language used. Use no stilted phrases, but remember that they are accustomed to the language of home, and talk to them in a sensible way. Do not attempt to overstrain the truth. Have respect to their spiritual condition. Remember they all need to believe in the Lord Jesus Christ, and that these little ones can and do love him. He preferred that the primary school be divided into classes.

On Wednesday evening Joseph Cook lectured on "Certainties in Religion." It is a pleasure to listen to him, as his lectures are packed full of thought, and he gives no uncertain sound. He charms his audience by his earnest words, and holds them closely to his line of argument for full two hours. The secular press of San Francisco abused him shamefully for his pronounced views on the Chinese question, but he stands deservedly high with the Christian community.

On Thursday evening there was a platform meeting, when addresses were made by a number of persons from the East and West, the farewell words were spoken, and the Assembly closed.

On Friday morning, July 4, we left Monterey, in company with Dr. Peltz, passing through the pleasant town of Salinas, where we stopped an hour, and then through the Salinas Valley to San Jose, where we left Dr. Peltz to pursue his journey to San Francisco, while we stopped over for a few days.

San Jose is one of the most beautiful towns I have seen in California, or, for that matter, anywhere. It has a population of about 15,000, has fine large streets, beautifully shaded, large business houses, and elegant private residences with beautiful grounds. There is an air of wealth and comfort about the place, and it looks as if the inhabitants expected to live here forever, so nicely have they fixed up their homes.

Santa Clara is three miles distant, and is connected with San Jose by street railways, one of which leads through the Alameda (The Beautiful Way), an avenue probably two hundred feet wide, shaded with magnificent trees. Santa Clara is almost a counterpart of San Jose. Here is the old Catholic mission church, built of adobe bricks, with walls fully four feet thick. The Jesuit College is also located in Santa Clara, the buildings and grounds inclosing eleven acres. Through the kindness of the chaplain, Father Leggia, I was shown through the various departments. The library contains 14,000 volumes, and is properly classified, containing books on religion, philosophy, history, politics, etc. Connected with the college is a business department, in which the students are taught banking, telegraphing, and all the various forms of business. There is also a large laboratory for the chemical students, a complete set of philosophical apparatus, a senate and house of representatives, in which the students are taught debating and parliamentary rules, and where laws are enacted, a chapel for the students, and a theatre which will hold 2,000 persons. They have a full orchestra, a brass band, and the students give private theatricals, to which their friends are invited. The students are not permitted outside the inclosure, and can only see their parents once a month.

Twelve miles south of San Jose is the Almaden Quicksilver Mine, owned by a New York company. They have seven furnaces, with a capacity for roasting 100 tons of ore daily. The ore is very rich in quicksilver, but the managers declined to give the percentage of metal to a ton. The ore is put into large furnaces, the mercury is driven off by heat, and passing through a series of condensers, runs into receivers, and is then put into large iron flasks, each holding 76½ pounds of mercury. They have a capacity for making 3,000 flasks monthly, and in June last shipped 1,600 flasks. They employ 500 men, who are paid $2.25 a day when working at the furnaces, and $2.00 a day when working in the yard. They work one month at the furnaces and one month in the yard, so as to prevent salivation, which frequently occurs. Sometimes they are so badly salivated that they cannot raise a hand to their mouths. Sulphur baths and a resort to the mountains are the remedies used.

There is a beautiful drive out Santa Clara street to the Alum Rock and Springs. The road is wide, smooth as a board, and for a distance of several miles is shaded with fine trees. It is six miles to the springs, which are up a canyon, whose rocky walls are shaded with oaks and pines. There are some half-dozen springs of alum, soda, iron and sulphur water, with their various combinations. Alum rock is about half a mile from the springs, and is said to contain a large percentage of alum. Leaving the springs we drove to the top of the hill, on which is located the fine residence of Gen. Smith, commanding a magnificent view of the Santa Clara Valley.

Fifty miles distant lies the bay of San Fancisco, shining in the noon-day sun like a sheet of burnished silver. The valley stretches out for miles before us, its brown fields relieved by patches of green, while almost at our feet is San Jose with its avenues of trees and variously-colored houses.

Near San Jose is Mt. Hamilton, where James Lick has directed an observatory to be built at a cost of half a million dollars.

As I said, it was the Fourth of July when I reached San Jose. The people celebrated it with quite a grand display. They had a tournament in which brave (?) knights clad in armor contended with each other for the privilege of crowning the queen of love and beauty, and a sham battle with all the pageantry of war. As a result, one man was killed by the premature explosion of a cannon, and another poor fellow had both hands blown off. It was a sad ending of the glorious Fourth, and cast a gloom over the community.

Through the kindness of the Rev. Dr. Calhoun, of the United Presbyterian Church, I had a drive around the city and visited the fine grounds and residence of Gen. Naglee. His grounds enclose about twenty-five acres within the city limits, are beautifully laid out, and contain trees and shrubbery of various kinds. The general is a native Pennsylvanian, a gentleman of the old school, and very hospitable. He has pronounced views on the Chinese question, and thinks they are the best laborers that can be employed. Several years ago about $75,000 worth of his property was destroyed by an incendiary fire because he would not discharge his Chinese laborers.

On Monday afternoon I took the cars for San Francisco, passing through Menlo Park, where the railroad and bonanza kings have their summer residences. It is a beautiful place, with its fine green lawns full of flowers, shrubbery and handsome residences, some of which cost $100,000 and upwards. By four o'clock we are in San Francisco, where we expect to spend a few days before turning our faces eastward.

NUMBER TWELVE.

CALIFORNIA—THE PEOPLE—GOOD-BYE—DAVISVILLE— FARMING—HARVESTING—LAKE TAHOE—OFF FOR VIRGINIA.

VIRGINIA CITY, JULY 16, 1879.

California is a wonderful State, rich in its mineral, agricultural and commercial wealth. The Californians are proud of their State, and enthusiastic in its praise, and no wonder. With its grand mountains rearing their lofty snow-clad summits until they seem to pierce the sky; with a valley whose granite walls stretch themselves heavenward nearly a mile, whose waterfalls are thousands of feet high, and whose grandeur is the wonder and admiration of the world; with a climate so delightful that the extreme heat of summer and the chilling blasts of winter are both unknown—a climate so invigorating and healthful that invalids rapidly gain strength, and not unfrequently are restored to health; with an extent of territory so great, that its shores for more than four hundred miles are washed by the Pacific ocean; with its cloudless, rainless skies from April to October, and its soil withal so productive that its fruits and cereals astonish the world. No wonder the Californian grows enthusiastic over his State and is loud in its praise. His pride is pardonable.

A gentleman, who has resided in the State some years, said to me you will find that here in California

"*Wealth* makes the man, and want of it the fellow,"

if for once I may change Pope. This may be true as to a certain class who look upon money as the potent and essential thing to give them a passport to society. We didn't find it so. The nature of our excursion was such as to throw us at once among the Christian people of the State. Coming among them as entire strangers, they at once opened their hearts and homes and bid us a cordial welcome, and entertained us right royally. Nowhere have I ever met with a more open-handed, generous and hospitable people than in California. This seems to be a characteristic of the people, for Mr. Hittell, in his "Resources of California," says: "It is perhaps partly on account of their State pride that Californians are cordial and hospitable. They want travelers to carry away good impressions of the country. The hospitality of the Californians is in keeping with their general mode of life. * * * They have traveled enough to know how to entertain and to accept entertainment."

The parson and your correspondent had an invitation to spend some time in the Sacramento Valley and take a look at California farming. On Saturday morning, July 12th, we bade good bye to San Francisco, he going by the overland route to Stockton, where he expected to see his brother, and your correspondent and a young lady, who was also to be a guest at the ranche, by way of Vallejo.

Taking the boat, we were soon steaming up the beautiful bay away from the city, and a few hours after were safely landed at Vallejo, where we took the cars and passed through a portion of the magnificent Napa Valley. Suddenly, without warning, we were plunged into darkness, and a few minutes thereafter emerge from the tunnel into daylight. We have passed through the Coast Range mountains, and from the Napa into the Sacramento Valley. At eleven o'clock we reach Davisville, thirteen miles west of Sacramento, and were met at the train by Mr. Greene, and driven five miles to his ranche. His farm contains nearly thirteen hundred acres, he maintaining that it is about as much land as one man can conveniently and profitably manage. His house is nicely located, surrounded with fine shade trees, and from the verandah you have a view of a portion of Sacramento and the State Capitol buildings, thirteen miles distant. We had an opportunity here of testing California hospitality to its utmost. We spent several days very pleasantly in this Christian home, and shall not forget the kindness of our host and hostess.

The San Joaquin and Sacramento Valleys are the great grain-growing region, and farming is carried on more extensively here than in any other portion of the State. The combined valleys are about four hundred miles in length and from forty to seventy in width. There are other valleys of note, as the Salinas, Sonoma, Santa Clara, Napa, and others, but none so large as these.

The principal cereals raised are wheat and barley, corn not doing well because of the dry climate! Whenever the ground is ready the farmer can sow his wheat, though it will not sprout until the autumn rains moisten the ground. The wheat will lie in the ground uninjured, as there is no danger to the seed. The farmers have discovered that a small quantity of blue vitriol mixed with the seed grain will prevent rust, and all seed is thus prepared before sowing. The vitriol is dissolved in water and mixed with the grain.

We had an opportunity of seeing the harvesters at work.

The grain is nearly all cut with a header—a machine that cuts the heads and about four inches of the stalk, leaving the straw on the field, which is then burned. From the header it is hauled to the thresher, which stands in the field, and is threshed and sacked ready for the market. It is no unusual thing to see large piles of grain in sacks out in the open field. The farmer takes it to his store-house when he gets time, for he does not fear rain.

Steam threshers are used to a considerable extent, but as there is great danger from fire where everything is so dry, they are at a discount with many farmers. We saw one field which was burned over and the grain destroyed by a spark from one of these machines. Thirteen hundred bushels is a day's threshing, and as the sacks hold about two and a half bushels, and are sewed shut, the sewer has very little time for looking about him.

The wheat yield, I was told, would average about thirty bushels to the acre. Four years ago, on Mr. Greene's farm, the average was forty-six and a half bushels. The average yield of barley is fifty bushels, though they occasionally get as much as eighty bushels to the acre. Mr. J. Bryant Hill, residing in the Salinas Valley, a few years ago raised one hundred and forty-seven and a half bushels of barley to the acre, but this was an exceptional yield.

While we were at the ranche they did a big day's work, threshing and sacking nineteen hundred and fifty bushels of barley in nine hours with a horse-power machine. It was an extraordinary day's work. A large derrick is erected over the machine, to which pulleys are attached, and four horses work two large forks which carry the grain to the man who feeds the machine, while the straw is taken from the machine by a boy and horse.

Tuesday evening, July 15th, we took the train at Davisville, bidding adieu to California and the friends whom we had met, and bearing their kind wishes for a safe journey. The next morning we are waked on the summit of the Sierra Nevada mountains, and catch a glimpse of Donner Lake, reflecting the mountains in its mirror-like surface. We speed down the grade, around the "mule shoe," and are safely landed at Truckee from which place we take the stage for the beautiful lake Tahoe.

The distance from Truckee to the lake is fourteen miles. The road leads along the Truckee river through the mountains, and is beautiful. The morning is bright and clear, and the air redolent with the odor of the pines. At every turn, something new is unfolded before you. Here a snow-capped mountain, there a dashing waterfall or a series of foaming cascades, then a rude mountain cabin with chubby children, who stop their swinging and their play to look at the passing stage, while again, farther on, some bold mountain peak comes prominently into view exposing its jagged, rocky side, when a sudden turn discloses a beautiful little valley, which seems to be playing hide-and-seek among these grand towering mountains.

At length we reach Tahoe City, containing less than a dozen houses, and before us, in its surpassing loveliness, bright, dazzling, beautiful, is Lake Tahoe, its soomth surface not rippled by a breeze. Two States claim ownership to the lake, as though it were too beautiful for one to monopolize. The State line between California and Nevada passes through it.

It is seven thousand feet above the sea, about twenty miles long and about half as broad, and looks like a great basin of molten silver, with the mountains, from three to four thousand feet high, for the rim. Beautiful! Magnificent! Grand! We might exhaust the list of adjectives and they would fail to decsribe it. You look into it, and, at a depth of fifty feet, see the bottom as plainly as though it were but five feet, while great speckled trout lounge lazily sunning themselves, or dart off in search of food. Sail across its clear bosom, and it changes continually like a chameleon.

Now it is dark indigo-blue; then again it is a light green; and again it is a clear white. The little steamer plows its way through the water, and the waves roll from its sides as if it was a sea of oil. The mountains are reflected in it as in a mirror, and its ever-changing color makes it marvelously beautiful.

The Niagara, a little steamer that looks more like a toy for children than a vessel to carry passengers, makes the circuit of the lake. We step aboard, the ropes are cast off, and we glide over the smooth surface of the water. The pulsations of the engine send a shiver through every timber of the little craft, but it scuds along over the water, and, charmed by the magnificent scenery, you are unmindful of the fact that the lake is eighteen hundred feet deep, and only a two-inch plank between you and the bottom.

In front of you is Job's Peak, 10,000 feet high, while on its right is Mount Tallac, 11,000 feet, its summit crowned with perpetual snow. To your right is Tinker's Nob, a cone-shaped rock, lifting its head 500 feet above the crest of the mountain.

We make the circuit of the lake, forty-four miles, and are landed at Glenbrook, where we take dinner, and are ready for a stage ride to Carson, the capital of Nevada.

Hank Monk, the driver who gave good old Horace Greeley his famous ride, can hardly wait for the passengers to get aboard. We have the stage held until we take a look at Shakspeare Rock, on which there is a fine head of the famous poet—so say those who knew him. We take their word for it, not having had the pleasure of his acquaintance. It is a perfect picture of somebody, and why not Shakspeare? Hank's patience is almost exhausted, and we bound into the stage and are off over the mountains, not caring to look down into the deep gorges along which we climb. Dust! Don't talk about it, for when you get to Carson you find that it isn't "all in your eye." Your eyes, your throat, your clothes—in fact everything is full of it.

Here we take the cars for Virginia City, the famous mining region of Nevada. The road winds around the mountains and is as crooked as a cork-screw. We pass a number of stamping mills, see a number of claims that have been prospected and staked off, pass through the town of Gold Hill, which you hardly see until you are on it, and where they now get only silver, and at last you are in Virginia City, which is built on the side of the mountain, about two thousand feet from the top and about the same distance from the bottom. Its streets run up the mountain and along its sides, and you climb with some difficulty two squares from the depot to the International Hotel, which is seven stories in front and five in the rear. After dining at eight o'clock you step out to see the city, but don't want to walk far over these hilly streets. It is growing late, too, and you have had a day's hard traveling, so you bid good-night to all the world and wait for morning to see the city and the mines.

NUMBER THIRTEEN.

VIRGINIA CITY—CHURCHES—DOWN IN A GOLD MINE— STAMPING—AMALGAMATING—ASSAYING.

DENVER, JULY 21, 1879.

"In early life Virginia City married a silver mountain and has wonderfully thriven since." Mountains crowd around it and are piled up in all directions. In the rear of the city Mount Davidson rises above its streets and houses to the height of a third of a mile, while away below the city, two thousand feet more, is the bottom of a canyon suggesting a possible way out to the open country. The city claims a population of about 25,000, fully one-half of whom live under the ground most of their time. It has some fine buildings, handsome stores which do a large business, and in which the goods are temptingly displayed for admiring

Virginians; several substantial bank buildings with elegant and commodious quarters for the officers and clerks, and great safes with ponderous doors which seem to smile complacently at would-be burglars and say, "We defy you." There are also numerous faro banks, how many I cannot tell, where the natives "fight the tiger" and do not come from the encounter without a scratch. These faro banks are not kept in some inaccessible place with barred and bolted door through which you cannot enter without assuring the porter, who peeps through the slide, that you are a "friend." We saw two of them in successful operation in one of the public rooms of the best hotel in the city.

Stock gambling is also carried on to a fearful extent. Many of the women, along with the men, having caught the mania, invest their little all in the hope of a rise and a fortune.

In October, 1875, a fire swept the city from end to end, destroying $10,000,000 of property, including all the mining works. Within sixty days all the principal mines had renewed their works, and within six months the city was rebuilt. In order to guard against a similar disaster an abundance of water has been introduced, brought thirty-one miles from Marlette's Lake, in the Sierras, at a cost of $2,000,000. But remember this water was brought for protection against fire, and is not the regular beverage of the average Virginian, as is evidenced by the numerous saloons seen everywhere, which are well patronized.

Religion is at a great discount here. The Presbyterians, Methodists and Baptists are represented, but neither church "does much business." A minister informed us that there were not more than two hundred religious people in the entire community, and he was quite sure he did not under-estimate it. In the morning when the gospel is preached, there is "a beggarly account of empty benches" in all the churches. In the evening some of the preachers deliver sensational sermons, taking such subjects as "old maids," "old bachelors," and the like, and of course they then have crowded houses.

It was to see Virginia and its mines, to go down into their deepest depths and explore their subterranean passages, to see the gold and silver bearing quartz, and the manner of separating the gold and silver from it, that took us to this metropolis of the young State of Nevada. We went, we saw, and we came away bearing in our pockets and in our hands the precious auriferous silver quartz, worth thousands of dollars a ton, thanks to the gentlemanly managers of the Consolidated Virginia and Savage mines. We want to tell you how it is mined and worked. Please, then, go with us down in a gold mine.

We were armed with a letter from Mr. Fish, President of the Consolidated Virginia, which had been transferred to us by our good brother Peltz, requesting the management to put us on the lowest level. As they were repairing a pump, they could not comply with the request, but directed us to Col. Gillett, superintendent of the Savage mine. He is a fine-looking, gentlemanly man, and if the mine is Savage the Colonel isn't. He directed the foreman to put us under ground with as much pleasure as relatives do a rich, childless old uncle. We were shown into a side-room, where we arrayed ourselves in clothing suitable for the mine. If it wasn't becoming, it had the merit of being serviceable. Thus attired, we were ready for the descent.

Giving each of us a lantern, we stepped on the platform over the mouth of the shaft. We had a rollicking Irishman for guide.

"Take hold of the railing, and keep your heads inside," he said.

"Ready," and at a signal from the foreman we felt as if the bottom of the universe had been knocked from under us, and we were dropping through illimitable space. It was a long time before we dared draw breath; how long I can't tell, but after an interminable time, we heard from out the gloom the cheery voice of our guide, and assurance returned. Away we flew; past shafts, past timbers, and Oh! how hot it was, as though they had some great furnace at the bottom and were going to roast us. At last we were going slower, and soon thereafter we stopped, having reached the bottom of the perpendicular shaft, 1,380 feet, *in less than two minutes!* How hot it is! One hundred and ten degrees! Whew! We pant for breath and our guide takes us to the air shaft where we are refreshed with the cool air. But we are not at the bottom. He pulls a signal rope and a car comes up. We are to descend 1,120 feet on an incline to the bottom of the mine. "Here are some gentlemen the Colonel sent down. Take good care of them," says this jovial son of Erin. We step into the car, the signal is given, and away we fly. "This is the Sutro tunnel," says our new guide, but we fly past the opening before he has said it. We reach the bottom, 2,000 feet from the surface, and pass off into the lateral shafts where men are at work, then come back into the cooling room, where they go for fresh air, and after having explored these lower regions are ready for the ascent.

"Will you let us see the Sutro tunnel?" we ask, as we step into the car.

He will. Away we fly for nearly a thousand feet, when our speed begins to slacken, and we stop, leave the car, and step on to a platform.

"Is this the tunnel?" we ask.

"No. This is our shaft leading into it. See, here is where we now pump our water," and raising a trap-door we saw the water rushing in.

"Before the completion of the Sutro tunnel we had to pump the water to the surface. Now we pump it to the 1,600 feet level, and it passes off through the tunnel. I'll take you there," and leading the way through a shaft several hundred yards, along the sides of which we could see the gray quartz rock, we came to a large opening. Descending about fifteen feet by a ladder, we stood in the famous Sutro tunnel running along this Comstock lode, which is, perhaps, the richest deposit of gold and silver bearing quartz in the world, as much as $23,000,000 having been taken from it in one year. The tunnel was made for the purpose of carrying off the water from the mines, and cost nearly or quite $5,000,000, and is fully four miles long.

We return, mount the car, and are whirled to the top of the incline. We thank our guide of the lower regions, promising if we meet any of his friends in Pennsylvania to bear them cheerful greetings, and resigning ourselves to the guardianship of our voluble guide with the "rich, Irish brogue," we are soon out of the shaft, into the open air, and breathe freer. A refreshing bath, and we are ready to follow the ore through its various processes of manipulation until it is turned into bricks of bullion.

Let us go to the Consolidated Virginia Mine to see how it is done. The quartz rock is raised from the mine in little cars. The machinery is of the most substantial character. The engines are large and powerful, and move smoothly and almost noiselessly, like a thing of life. When a car comes to the surface it is pushed on a track, railroaded to the stamping mill and dumped into shutes which carry the ore to the stamps. These are arranged in rows, and the rock is fed to them very regularly. They keep up a terrible clatter, but the heavy iron pestles descend with a force that means business. A continuous stream of water is poured into the mortars, which washes the finely powdered quartz through the meshes of a seive into a large flume which carries it to the pan mill, about a quarter of a mile distant. Here it flows into large tanks where the dust settles to the bottom and the water runs off. It is then put into pans, which are great iron hoppers holding 3,000 pounds each, and ground for three hours until it is an impalpable powder. Three hundred and forty pounds of mercury are then added, and the grinding continued two hours longer, when the gold and silver unite with the mercury and form an amalgam. After being thus ground it is run into what are anomalously called "settlers," where it is kept in continuous agitation for two and a half hours longer, when it is drawn off into large canvas bags through which a portion of the mercury filters, leaving the amalgam behind. The amalgam is a white unctuous mass which you can press in your hand like soft putty. From the strainers it is transferred to a large iron pan and washed with a solution of cyanide of potassium and water, which removes all the dirt. It is next put into a hydraulic press, holding sixteen hundred pounds, the pressure is applied, and six hundred pounds of the quicksilver is forced out. Of the remaining one thousand pounds of amalgam, three-fourths is mercury. We now follow it to the retorts, which are similar to those used in gas works, and will each hold a ton of the amalgam. The retorts are tightly closed in front, but have an opening at the back part, with a pipe leading to a cold water condenser. Intense heat is applied, the mercury is volatilized, driven off and condensed under water, while the crude bullion, which in appearance resembles pipe clay, is left behind in a mass. This is then taken to the assaying room, where it is put into large crucibles, borax is added for a flux, and the dross rising to the surface is skimmed off, leaving the pure metal, which is run into bricks weighing 2,000 ounces, and are worth $5,000 each when they contain gold and silver, and $2,000 each when only silver. In order to separate the gold from the silver, the bricks are placed in sulphuric acid and boiled. The silver combines with the acid, forming sulphate of silver, and the gold is set free. The sulphate of silver is then run over plates of copper, the acid uniting with the copper forms sulphate of copper, and the silver is liberated.

The assaying room is one of very great interest. The machinery is of the most delicate kind. They have scales which weigh 5,000 ounces, and yet they are so constructed that the hundredth part of an ounce will turn them. We saw a small scale which weighs the twenty-five hundredths of an ounce.

Great accuracy is required, as the smallest proportion of a grain will make a difference of $50 to $60 in determining the value of a brick.

Every ton of ore is assayed to find its value, and must produce that amount of precious metal so that there can be no stealing done by any of the workmen. A half ounce of the crushed quartz is used for making the assay. The quartz is put into a crucible with some borax, soda and litharge, thence into a furnace and heated. A lead button is formed, the gold and silver uniting with the lead in the litharge. This lead button is next put in a small cupel, made of bone dust, and placed in the furnace. The cupel absorbs the base metal, leaving the gold and silver in the form of a small globule, varying in size from a pin's head to that of a pea, according to the quantity of precious metal contained in the ore. This is put into acid, the one separated from the other, and the quantity of each of the precious metals is thus obtained. The whole process of assaying and finding the value of the ore, is one requiring skill and a thorough acquaintance with the science of analysis. The ore taken from the same mine varies in value, and is worth "from nothing to five thousand dollars a ton," as we were informed.

We are under many obligations to Mr. Taylor, Mr. Elder, the chief assayer, and Mr. Shaw, all of the Virginia mine, for much valuable information, many favors, and the fine specimens of quartz rock which we were enabled to carry away with us.

Having seen the mines, the ore, the machinery, the process of extracting the gold and silver, and having "done" Virginia, we were ready to shake its dust from our feet, and turn our faces eastward again. We step aboard the cars, bid farewell to the city and its bonanza mines, and are off again over this cork-screw of a railroad which winds in and out, among and around the mountains, and at last are safely landed in Carson. We stop here only a few minutes, and are then off again for Reno, which we reach at nine o'clock, and where *we* must wait until three the next morning for the overland express. We will leave *you* waiting here another week before we resume our journey.

NUMBER FOURTEEN.
HOMEWARD—OGDEN—CHEYENNE TO DENVER—COLORADO SPRINGS—CHEYENNE CANYON—GARDEN OF THE GODS—PIKE'S PEAK—IOWA—HOME.

Lebanon, Pa., August 29, 1879.

"Wake me early in the morning, at the first break of day,"
are the words which have been put into the mouth of poor old Nicodemus, a "slave of African birth." He wanted to be waked for the great jubilee of freedom. We reached Reno on the night of July 17th, and wanted to be waked early for the overland express, which left at 3 o'clock in the morning.

Long before the day had any thought of breaking we were down stairs and out in the darkness. We found the train already there, and stepping aboard the cars, were soon whirling eastward. When day finally broke, and the passengers were astir, we found our friends whom we had left at Lake Tahoe, and in addition thereto, our friend Ed. S. Wagoner, Secretary of the Pennsylvania State Sunday-school Association, and his party, so that there were no less than sixteen of the Pacific Pilgrims on the train, all of whom were homeward bound, and who, with two exceptions, expected to spend some time in seeing the sights in Colorado.

We also had Francis Murphy, who was on his way from San Francisco, where he had been engaged in temperance work, having secured about eight thousand signers to the pledge. We found him to be a genial Irishman, whose company we enjoyed.

We are now on the Nevada desert, with sage brush as the only sign of vegetation. Near one of the stations we saw two tramps lying on the sand, with the sun pouring his burning rays into their faces. They were sleeping soundly, totally oblivious to all surrounding circumstances. Their hands and faces looked as though they had not seen water for an age. I have sometimes envied these fellows their delightful leisure, and their entire freedom from the cares of business, but having had a long vacation, my feelings were those of pity and disgust.

About nine o'clock we reached Humboldt, a delightful spot of green in this great Desert. Here, by a system of irrigation, the desert has been made to blossom as the rose. The beautiful verdure, and the babbling fountain in front of the hotel, were a relief after the sand and alkali of the plains. We pass other places of interest where we had receptions by the citizens and Sunday-schools on our way west, and reach Ogden on Saturday morning at 8 o'clock. Here the Central and Union Pacific roads meet and shake hands over the spoils of the travelers. They have entered in a compact to remain united, and this alliance is mutually profitable to all concerned, as the plethoric pocket-books of the management and stockholders abundantly attest. We had to wait here two hours for time to get even, as the one road runs by San Francisco and the other by Omaha time.

At length we are off, and from this point to Evanston we pass some of the most magnificent scenery on the road, which has been described in our letter westward. The time is passed most delightfully with such pleasant company. In the afternoon we had a court trial, and as we were near Wyoming, where women vote and hold office, we had a lady for judge. Witnesses were heard, the case argued, and "her honor" rendered the decision. The sentence was severe, the sex of the judge, perhaps, having something to do with its severity. Some of us had thought of running down to Salt Lake City and spending Sabbath there, but as the majority wanted to go on and spend Sunday somewhere in the mountains, we concluded to pursue our journey eastward with the party. But where shall we stop? was the question. As night came we could find no place that seemed suitable, and so we concluded to run on to Denver, even though we would have to travel on Sabbath.

Sunday morning we had a most delightful service on the train, conducted by Mr. Wagoner, and participated in by a number of the tourists. We felt that though we could find no suitable place to stop and spend Sunday in worship, we could still honor God by this service on the cars.

On Sabbath afternoon our train stopped on the plains, near a natural soda spring and gave all an opportunity of tasting the water. It is strongly impregnated with soda, and on the ground around the spring there is quite a deposit of the salt, the result of the evaporation of the water.

Farther on we saw a herd of antelope quietly grazing near the road. As the cars passed they raised their heads, looked at us without evincing the least astonishment or fear, and then resumed their eating.

At 3 o'clock we reached Cheyenne where we changed cars for Denver, one hundred and thirty-five miles distant by rail. You must leave the line of the Union Pacific railroad, as we learned, if you would see the Rocky Mountains in all their grandeur. The

scenery from Cheyenne to Denver is beautiful. On our right were
the mountains, peak after peak rising, the one above the other,
while Long's Peak stood high over all, like a watchful sentinel on
duty. On our left were the broad and fertile plains of Wyoming,
where large bands of horses and great herds of cattle roamed at
pleasure or grazed undisturbed, except by the shrill whistle of the
locomotive. The prairie dogs, cute little fellows that they are, sat
erect and looked at us so comically, or scampered off to their homes
as fast as they could, doubtless feeling a sense of security there. We
reach the Cache la Poudre Valley, a beautiful fertile tract of country, watered by a river of the same name. An abundance of cotton-
wood and box elder grow along the stream, while the ripening
grain and growing corn give abundant evidence of the fertility of
the soil. Boulder, Longmont, Golden, and other towns are passed,
and at 9 o'clock at night we are safely landed in Denver, the capital of the State. The city claims a population of 30,000. Its streets
are laid out at right angles, are fine and wide, with rows of trees
shading the sidewalks, and lending additional beauty to the surrounding scenery. It is a pretty city, has some elegant buildings,
fine large stores, and does a great deal of business, being the principal source of supply for the surrounding towns and mining regions.
The arrivals for the week were nearly three thousand, many of
whom came to stay, while others, like ourselves, were there as
tourists.

Tuesday morning (July 22), we left by the Denver and Rio
Grande railroad for Colorado springs, seventy-five miles farther
south. The Rio Grande is a narrow-gauge road, with Denver as its
northern, and Alamosa, on the Rio Grande river, as its southern
terminus. The road runs close to the mountains, which have a peculiar blue tint when seen from a distance, but as we approach
them, this changes and you see the red color of the soil, and find
they have comparatively little verdure. The sunlight as it filtered
through the clouds, gives them a glorious coloring of light and shade
which an artist might well envy to depict.

Our route for Colorado was laid out by the Rev. Dr. Sheldon
Jackson, superintendent of Presbyterian missions in the West. He

was with our excursion, resides in Denver, and is thoroughly familiar with the resorts in Colorado. By following his directions we were enabled to see many places of interest and economize time and money.

Why Colorado Springs is thus named we were unable to learn, as the springs are at Manitou, six miles distant. The town was laid out in 1871, and now claims a population of 5,000, one-half of whom, I suppose, are invalids. There is no liquor sold in the place, and no licenses are granted. The deeds to the property exclude the sale of intoxicants forever on the premises, under a penalty of forfeiture.

On the afternoon of our arrival we visited Cheyenne Canyon, about five miles from the town. The canyon is a deep gorge in the mountain, through which a stream tortuously finds its way, forming a series of magnificent falls and cascades from the time it leaves its home in the mountain top to the open plain below.

At the entrance of the canyon some fellow, poetically inclined, thus advertises:

> "While your horse the herbage munches,
> Turn in here and get your lunches;
> Butter, and eggs, and bread—home-made,
> Iced cream, milk and lemonade;
> Coffee and tea, also, you'll find,
> Eat, drink, and through the canyon wind."

A path leads along the stream, and once in the canyon you are enclosed on every side by high perpendicular walls. You wind along the stream, and as you turn and look back, the way out seems impassible, as though some Titan had blockaded your pathway with an immense wall of stone. Half a mile up the canyon we come to a series of waterfalls which are magnificent, the water falling about fifty feet, and twisted very peculiarly in its descent. The scenery is weird and wild, and you return satisfied with one of the attractions of Colorado.

Glen Eyrie, with its massive rocks, its wealth of foliage, cascades, and, above all, its Major Domo, a needle-like rock one hundred feet in height, which might well be called Cleopatra's Needle, present scenery beautiful enough for the pencil of an artist.

The Garden of the Gods is the most striking of all the peculiar rock formations. The entrance is formed by two ledges of rock, which are three hundred and fifty feet in height. Between these there is an opening probably sixty feet wide, in the centre of which stand Jupiter and Juno, two immense rocks from seventy-five to one hundred feet high, who seem to be the guardians of the garden. The rocks present various forms, some of them of the most grotesque character. Photograph Rock bears on its face a stag's head, a man's arm with clenched fist, and an ape's face, all of which are natural formations of red stone in grey rock. The Polar Rock, Seal and Nun, Pisa's leaning tower, Mother Grundy, Laughing Dutchman, the Balancing Rock and others, are most wonderful formations.

From the Garden we drove to Manitou Springs. Here several hotels are erected, and it has become quite a famous health resort. The waters are iron and soda, with both of which they are very strongly charged. The Leadville road passes the springs, and leads through Ute Pass, which is well worth a visit. Large teams with heavily laden wagons slowly toil up the mountain road, alongside of which, hundreds of feet below, is a stream that in descending forms a number of waterfalls, the finest of which is Rainbow Falls.

We return to Colorado Springs by noon, for we have arranged for the greatest of all excursions, the ascent of Pike's Peak, and are to leave in the afternoon, reach the Lake House, four miles from the top, remain there all night, and make the ascent in the morning. Promptly on time "Old Marsh of Pike's Peak" (he can't deny the name, for it was distinctly lettered on the back of his coat in white paint,) was on hand with the "Donkey train," and seven as jolly tourists as you ever saw were ready. Our party consisted of four ladies and three gentlemen, and comprised an artist, a historian, a traveled lady, a poet, a parson, a funny man and a correspondent. As we looked at the diminutive donkeys, which bore the euphonious names of Tom, Jerry, Dick, Muldoon, Rarus, Wild Cat, Greaser, Jennie and Jack, one of which carried large tin panniers, containing the lunch, the question arose whether we should carry them, or they us. On Marsh's assurance that it was all right, we mounted and *slowly* wended our way toward the mountain amid the smiles and good wishes of the people who had gathered to see us off. The funny man declared that my donkey's ears only were visible. We went by the Bear Creek trail, nineteen miles from the springs to the top. The trail wound up a deep canyon, but the time passed pleasantly, for something new was being continually unfolded before us. When we had attained an elevation of about nine thousand feet a storm came down on us. It was fearfully grand! The lightning flashed, almost blinding us by its nearness and it brilliancy, and the thunder rolled from peak to peak, until the reverberations were lost in the distance. The grandeur of such a thunder storm cannot be described. In about an hour the rain ceased and a stream of sunlight poured down through the canyon. A beautiful rainbow spanned the chasm from mountain to mountain, while every leaf and bush and spear of grass sparkled as though studded with brilliant gems.

We reached the Lake House in the dusk of the evening, tired and wet, and were glad to enjoy the warm welcome of the generous stove. In looking over the register we found that our old friend, Isaac Frazer, member of the Board of Publication, and his son, E. K. Frazer, were here June 2, 1879, but could not get to the summit, as the snow was five feet deep. We were going to the summit, and for once I thought I would be ahead of my good brother Frazer.

The next morning we started for the summit of the Peak. At an elevation of 12,000 feet we were above the timber line. Vegetation was scant, but beautiful mountain flowers were in bloom in this high altitude. The donkeys stepped very carefully and slowly, and our poet, who was in the rear, fell away behind the rest and was observed to be busy with note book and pencil. When we reached the top and were enjoying the lunch, we were favored with the following which I will embalm for posterity:

"If ever I go to Pike's Peak again,
  I'll be sure to go by the donkey train,
  For the Donkey train the desire implants
  To take all your sisters, and your cousins, and your aunts.

"I like to ride on a donkey small,
  For he steps so slow that he doesn't fall;
  His step is sure as an elephant's,
  And he'll carry all your sisters, and your cousins, and your aunts.

"The donkey's little, but he's very strong;
  His feet are small, and his ears are long;
  His voice is musical, and he beautifully chants,
  Like any fellow's sisters, and his cousins, and his aunts.

"And, now, please pardon this little freak,
  Of rhyming as I'm climbing to the top of Pike's Peak;
  The peak whose trail the tourist's vision haunts,
  Along with his sisters, and his cousins, and his aunts."

A ride over rocks and snow, and, hurrah! here we are, on the top of Pike's Peak, 14,147 feet above the ocean! The least exertion is tiresome, the pulse is quickened, and beats life away at a fearfully rapid rate—an average of 120 pulsations per minute.

The government has a signal station erected here, and we were told the greatest velocity of the wind was 108 miles an hour, and the greatest cold 37 degrees below zero. The average temperature for the year was 18 degrees. In winter the signal men go up and down on snow-shoes.

The view from the top is impressive, bounded only by the horizon and the clouds. Away off in the distance was the Arkansas Valley, with the river barely distinguishable. Mountain peaks were piled behind and on top of each other, as though the Almighty hand had shaken them from cloudland, and they had fallen in one confused mass. Deep gorges lay at our feet, into which we looked with a shudder, while away off stretched the valley of the Colorado, with the springs in the distance. After two hours we were ready to return. Away off to our left the clouds had gathered, and from out their darkness we saw vivid lightning flashes. We reached the Lake House, where we rested a few minutes, and then continued our descent, the storm all the while preceding us. When we had descended five thousand feet we found great quantities of hail in the pathway, and when we reached Colorado Springs, about 8 o'clock, we were informed that one of the heaviest storms they had for years had just preceded us. We were most fortunate in escaping its fury. We were glad to retire early, after twenty-three miles of mountain climbing on such slow going animals as donkeys.

Pike's Peak was discovered in 1844, by Col. Pike of the U. S. A., whilst on an exploring expedition up the Arkansas river. The Peak was named in his honor. The first persons who ever ascended it were some of Fremont's party, among them Kit Carson, about 1848–9. The Pike's Peak gold discovery was made by a Frenchman, Joe DeFecto, in the year 1857. Joe was *defect-ive* in his judgment, for his gold proved to be iron pyrites. Gold, however, was found on Camp Creek, and in Cherry Creek, at what is now Denver. In 1858 the great excitement and rush began. In 1862 gold was found in California Gulch, near what is now Leadville; and proved to be very rich. My informant told me that he and two others took out $9,000 worth of dust in three months.

Friday, July 25th, we bade our lady friends good-bye and returned to Denver, where we remained until Monday, when we started eastward. We reached Omaha on Tuesday afternoon, and by nine o'clock were in Denison, thirty miles south of Ida, where our friends Kolp and Kennedy reside, whom we had promised to visit on our return.

A ride across the prairies, where we lost our way several times, brought us, about ten o'clock, to the farm of Brother Kennedy. He has fourteen hundred acres of as fine land as you can see any where, seven hundred of which are under cultivation. He was in the midst of harvest, and two of M'Cormick's self-binding harvesters were cutting the stalks of well-filled grain. Bro. Kennedy was in good health, has developed into a first-class farmer, and is enjoying life in his new, western home.

After dinner we drove over to the home of our good Brother Kolp. He, too, is nicely fixed. He has the finest house we saw between Denison and Ida. It commands a view of the town, two miles

ACROSS THE CONTINENT. 97

distant, the railroad and a large portion of the surrounding country. David was busy at work cutting grain, and looked like an old farmer, and not like the active, pushing merchant, as when he was in Harrisburg. He has 480 acres of land, only 160 acres in the farm where he resides. Brother Kolp is enjoying good health. Mrs. Kolp and the children are in excellent health and like their new home. We spent the night with him, and after we returned from Ida, at 10 o'clock at night, we hitched the horses in the harvester and cut an acre of oats, your correspondent driving and David working the machine.

The country about Ida is beautiful. It would be hard to find better land anywhere, suitable alike for farming or grazing. Nearly every farm has a stream of water, and the soil is of that rich prairie loam that is so productive.

On our way to Denison, we stopped to see the family of Brother George Yousling, who has just moved into the country. Sister McFadden is with them. They were all well, and though their home is new and so entirely different from Harrisburg, they doubted not they would like it equally as well after they were rightly settled.

There are quite a number of church members here, and the Iowa Eldership should look after our church interests in this locality.

Leaving Denison, at 9 o'clock at night, by 4 o'clock of Friday, August 1st, we were in Chicago, which place we left the same evening. On Saturday afternoon we were among the mountains of Pennsylvania, and felt at home once more. The mountains of Pennsylvania are in striking contrast with those of the far West. The Sierra Nevada and Rocky Mountains are grand and majestic; the Alleghanies are beautiful. The pine, spruce and fir, mingling with the oaks, present a contrast of coloring that is magnificent, while from base to summit they are covered with a luxuriant growth of timber.

At 11 o'clock at night we step from the cars in the city of Harrisburg, and the next morning at six, reach Lebanon, after an absence of a little more than ten weeks.

Our Pacific excursion was ended. Many pleasant acquaintances were formed *en route* and in California, all of whom will be remembered with pleasure. A kind Providence watched over me, and not an hour's sickness, or detention, or any accident marred the pleasure of the trip. To Him I give heartfelt thanks. To the tourists and friends whom I met, and from whom I received so many kindnesses, and to the readers for their kind indulgence as I have tried to take them with me "Across the Continent," I return my thanks and kind wishes.

www.ingramcontent.com/pod-product-compliance
Lightning Source LLC
Chambersburg PA
CBHW020901160426
43192CB00007B/1019